UNDERSTANDING
THE BEATS

Understanding Contemporary American Literature

Matthew J. Bruccoli,
Editor

UNDERSTANDING
THE
BEATS

EDWARD HALSEY FOSTER

UNIVERSITY OF SOUTH CAROLINA PRESS

Published in Columbia, South Carolina, by the
University of South Carolina Press

Manufactured in the United States of America

Foster, Edward Halsey.
     Understanding the Beats / Edward Halsey Foster.
          p.   cm.—(Understanding contemporary American literature)
     Includes bibliographical references and index.
     ISBN 0–87249–798–4 (hardcover; alk. paper)
     ISBN 0–87249–878–6 (paperback)
     1. American literature—20th century—History and criticism.
2. Beat generation.   I. Title   II. Series.
PS228.B6F67
810.9'0054—dc20   91-36122

For

Katherine Hearn Foster

and

John Clark Foster

CONTENTS

EDITOR'S PREFACE

Understanding Contemporary American Literature has been planned as a series of guides or companions for students as well as good nonacademic readers. The editor and publisher perceive a need for these volumes because much of the influential contemporary literature makes special demands. Uninitiated readers encounter difficulty in approaching works that depart from the traditional forms and techniques of prose and poetry. Literature relies on conventions, but the conventions keep evolving; new writers form their own conventions—which in time may become familiar. Put simply, *UCAL* provides instruction in how to read certain contemporary writers—identifying and explicating their material, themes, use of language, point of view, structures, symbolism, and responses to experience.

The word *understanding* in the series title was deliberately chosen. Many willing readers lack an adequate understanding of how contemporary literature works; that is, what the author is attempting to express and the means by which it is conveyed. Although the criticism and analysis in the series have been aimed at a level of general accessibility, these introductory volumes are meant to be applied in conjunction with the works they cover. Thus they do not provide a substitute for the works and authors they introduce, but rather prepare the reader for more profitable literary experiences.

M.J.B.

PREFACE

Poetry is the record of individual insights into the secret soul of the individual—and, because all individuals are One in the eyes of their Creator, into the soul of the World.

—Allen Ginsberg,
"Poetry, Violence, and the Trembling Lambs"

According to the back cover of a paperback edition, Jack Kerouac's *On the Road* (1957) "turned on a whole generation to the youthful subculture that was about to crack the gray facade of the fifties wide open and begin the greening of America." The rhetoric is extravagant, and what it says may be true—but it was certainly not what Kerouac himself wanted. For him the book was a serious literary endeavor and obviously not the guide for the superficially alienated that, in effect, it very soon became.

The Beats did not need academics or critics to establish their reputations. As the country moved away from the contained, conservative temperament of the postwar period, they became celebrities, and, like all celebrities, they were dependent for their reputations on newspapers, magazines, and television. When the temperament of the country again became conservative, journalists turned to other subjects and people, but many university English departments now had instructors for whom Allen Ginsberg and not, for example, Richard Wilbur or John Crowe Ransom was a major poet. As poet and novelist Keith Abbott wrote in "Ballad of Jack Kerouac's 1957," Kerouac's defenders included "a buncha professors who once took acid." There is now an enormous critical literature on the Beats, and

Preface

Ginsberg's "Howl" is conventionally found in anthologies for college American literature survey courses.

It may be just as well that the Beats are no longer the celebrities they once were. Their famé assured that they would be read, yet they were perhaps better known for their personalities and the values they represented than for their books. Confusing the writer with the subject of *On the Road,* Kerouac's early followers were surprised to find that he did not even like to drive. They never understood that his real revolution had to do with language.

This book provides a general introduction to the four major beat writers—William S. Burroughs, Gregory Corso, Allen Ginsberg, and Jack Kerouac. Sometimes those with whom they were later associated (Gary Snyder, Michael McClure, Lawrence Ferlinghetti, and Robert Creeley, among others) are considered Beats, but when the term is used that way, it becomes too general to be of much significance. Burroughs, Corso, Ginsberg, and Kerouac were closely allied at the beginning of their careers and shared a particular vision of America—a vision which in turn defined much of their most celebrated work.

They wrote in reaction to the materialistic, conformist America they saw developing in the 1940s. In part that America was an understandable response to an era of economic depression and war, but that brave new world also seemed a very repressive culture—to the Beats, indeed, a police state—and this recognition dominates their work.

Their object was to find a way out of that world, and their means were fiction and poetry. Literature allowed the writer to see things as they were while at the same time providing an entry into transcendent realities. The best-known

Preface

beat works—"Howl," *Naked Lunch, On the Road*—
respond directly to social and political conditions at mid-
century while indicating ways to escape from them.

The first chapter of this book considers the Beats'
shared political, social, and literary concerns, particularly
the hipster values they encountered in New York during the
1940s. Each writer is then discussed individually with particular attention to ways in which his work responded personally, aesthetically, and politically to those concerns. A
concluding chapter suggests briefly the range of beat influence on later writers and the place of beat poetry and fiction in the context of recent experimental writing.

My debt to friends and colleagues is large. Many
times this study shifted direction as the result of discussions
with others. I would like to thank particularly Joseph Don-
ahue, Michael McClure, Alice Notley, and Philip Whalen.
Earlier discussions with Clark Coolidge, Simon Pettet, and
Anne Waldman in many ways helped to clarify my sense of
beat aesthetics. My debt to Ted Berrigan is too great to be
expressed; in a very real way, he changed everything.
George Wedge read a portion of the manuscript, and his
criticisms are appreciated. The staffs of the Bancroft Library at the University of California, Berkeley, and the Columbia University Library provided invaluable assistance.
But the greatest debt, of course, is to Katherine, John, and,
above all, Elaine, who are the real saints.

UNDERSTANDING
THE BEATS

CHAPTER ONE

Hipsters, Beats, and the True Frontier

The fluency and ornaments of the finest poems . . . are not independent but dependent. All beauty comes from beautiful blood and a beautiful brain.

—Walt Whitman,
Preface to *Leaves of Grass*

The Beats, according to an article in *Life* magazine in 1959, were "the only rebellion around."[1] Whether their fiction and poetry altered the way people thought or merely reflected social and cultural change, the Beats were responsible for some of the most powerful writing in America at that time. As significant as the Beats may have been to American social history at mid-century, their books were their principal achievement.

There are four major beat writers: William S. Burroughs, Gregory Corso, Allen Ginsberg, and Jack Kerouac. Others with whom they were associated and who strongly affected their work—Neal Cassady, Herbert Huncke, and Carl Solomon, for example—were not as committed to writing as were the original four. Still others like Alan Ansen and John Clellon Holmes, although they dealt with similar materials and ideas, were stylistically more conservative and less adventurous.

In the late 1950s and early 1960s, journalists included several other writers among the Beats—Gary Snyder, Philip Whalen, Michael McClure, William Everson, and Lawrence Ferlinghetti, among others—but, as most of these writers themselves quickly pointed out, that was a mistake. Philip Whalen, for example, insisted that the word *beat* involved "a period in New York City that Allen and Jack and Clellon Holmes and Burroughs and Corso and many other people were involved in. I wasn't there. . . . I don't think of myself as a 'beat.' "[2]

The confusion arose initially from the fact that various beat writers were living in the Bay Area during the San Francisco Renaissance, that sudden flowering of poetry (and audiences for poetry) in San Francisco in the 1950s. Journalists, unable to distinguish between, say, Ginsberg's poems and Whalen's, decided that anyone who lived and wrote in North Beach must be part of the same revolution, and soon America thought so, too. Some academics also identified the Beats largely with writers associated in some way with San Francisco. Thomas Parkinson, for example, pointed out that San Francisco had developed its own characteristic poetry long before Ginsberg and Kerouac arrived there, yet he included Ferlinghetti, Snyder, Whalen, and McClure among the Beats in his influential 1961 anthology of poetry and criticism, *A Casebook on the Beat.*[3]

San Francisco poets, however, have continued to resist the label. Gary Snyder said that *beat* could be used in "[talking] about the overall social phenomenon," but that "as a poet I belong to the San Francisco renaissance; . . . I'm not a Beat poet." In fact, he has said, "I never did know exactly what was meant by the term 'The Beats.' " Ferlinghetti has insisted that he was not in any way influenced by the Beats and turned down the opportunity to publish *Naked Lunch* "because I didn't like that kind of writing."[4]

Hipsters, Beats, and the True Frontier

McClure's plays and poetry have little in common with Burroughs's fiction, and Snyder's aesthetics are very different from Ginsberg's. The word *beat* can too easily be appropriated to describe a range of experimental or innovative poets and novelists with little else in common except a general resistance to academic poetry and to conservative values and politics in America during the 1950s.

If one is talking, however, about the "Beat Generation" as a sociological rather than as a literary movement, then Snyder, McClure, Whalen, and so forth might be grouped with Burroughs, Corso, Ginsberg, and Kerouac. Over the years, McClure, for example, has adamantly insisted that, strictly speaking, he was never a Beat, although he could be included as one "in the broadest sense." In that case, however, Robert Creely and other Black Mountain poets should be included as well.[5] Ann Charters suggested the larger spectrum in *The Beats* (1983), which includes essays even on such writers as William Carlos Williams, Frank O'Hara, and Jack Spicer, who were in no sense Beats themselves but who influenced, or were at least aware of and criticized (quite negatively in Spicer's case), the work of those who were.

The word *beat* in the larger sense might also include writers from the 1960s such as Diane di Prima, LeRoi Jones (Amiri Baraka), Ed Sanders, Clark Coolidge, and Anne Waldman—writers, that is, whose poetry and fiction were influenced by the Beats or were at least similar to theirs. At that point, however, one is including a very large portion of contemporary innovative or avant-garde writers—so large in fact that the word again loses precision. It is better in this case to talk about a second generation.

Understanding the Beats

Whalen was correct in locating the Beats geographically in New York, for it was there in the 1940s that their politics and literary ambitions were formed. Burroughs, Corso, Ginsberg, and Kerouac were friends long before they published anything of consequence. Kerouac and Ginsberg knew each other as undergraduates at Columbia, and Burroughs met them both in 1944. Ginsberg met Corso six years later in 1950 and introduced him shortly afterward to Kerouac. The circle was complete in 1953 when Burroughs, who had been living in Mexico, returned to New York and met Corso. These four writers shared a set of experiences at a crucial moment in their lives (and, for that matter, in the course of American civilization) and developed political and social visions that often overlapped. They wrote about each other, solicited each other's criticism, and promoted each other's books. If in the end they seem very different writers (and even Burroughs himself has said, "You couldn't really find four writers more different, more distinctive"[6]), their careers did intersect at a crucial moment, giving them a shared perspective and sensibility.

These four writers are in many ways so distinctively individual that at times it may seem as if the entire beat phenomenon were nothing but a journalist's or a critic's fantasy. Nonetheless, when one puts the fiction and poetry of the Beats next to, for example, the work of John Updike, Saul Bellow, William Bronk, William Gaddis, John Barth, Robert Lowell, Anne Sexton, or even Gary Snyder and Michael McClure, among other writers who emerged as major figures between the end of World War II and the mid-1960s, it is clear that the Beats do comprise a separate

group, not only because they strongly encouraged and influenced each other aesthetically but also because they
shared a particular attitude, largely urban and Eastern in
origin, about what they felt had gone wrong with America.
As Corso said, "the beats that I really knew, Kerouac,
Ginsberg, Burroughs, they were all very diverse in their
writing styles, but," he adds, "there was a similarity . . .
with their feeling of what was coming, of what was to be."[7]

Burroughs was much older than the other Beats,[8] and,
unlike them, he was not at first interested in becoming a
writer. It was Kerouac, he said, who encouraged him to
write. Kerouac was obsessed with becoming a writer but
had read much less than Burroughs. Columbia taught Ginsberg and Kerouac the classics, but Burroughs showed them
what had been left out—Hart Crane, T. S. Eliot, Céline,
Kafka, Cocteau, Spengler, and other modern writers.

Kerouac and Ginsberg met Burroughs through Lucien
Carr, a fellow Columbia student with whom they discussed the possibility of a "New Vision"—a new way of
understanding the world. This Rimbaud-like enterprise was
certainly abetted by the kind of books Burroughs recom-
mended and the people with whom he associated. Here was
an equivocal realm of petty thieves and addicts, in some
ways like the inhabitants of Céline's Paris, who constituted
a largely self-sufficient world indifferent to conventional
values and ideals. Here also were the beginnings of "hip"
culture—the world of the hipster, which began to form in
New York and other cities toward the end of the war.

The hipster, in Norman Mailer's classic definition, set
out "to encourage the psychopath in oneself, to explore
that domain of experience where security is boredom and

therefore sickness, and one exists in the present, in that enormous present which is without past or future, memory or planned intention, the life where a man must go until he is beat, where he must gamble with his energies through all those small or large crises of courage and unforeseen situations which beset his day, where he must be with it or doomed not to swing."[9]

The hipster, said Mailer, knows that "new kinds of victories increase one's power for new kinds of perception; and defeats, the wrong kinds of defeats, attack the body and imprison one's energy until one is jailed in the prison air of other people's habits, other people's defeats, boredom, quiet desperation, and muted icy self-destroying rage."[10] Although hipsters were a national phenomenon, they were usually found in cities. Most of the other writers later associated with the Beats were at this time living abroad or in small cities and towns, and although they could not fail to encounter hipsters somewhere (for the cultural influence was seen from jazz to movies to the way people dressed), it would have been difficult to know the type as well or as intensely as Burroughs, Ginsberg, and Kerouac did. These writers were there, so to speak, at the creation, watching from Times Square as this new cultural force took shape, and all three, in their very different ways, adopted in their works an attitude and outlook that was unmistakably hip. Corso during these years was living on New York streets or in foster homes or in prison and absorbed the same sensibility more directly.

Burroughs introduced Kerouac and Ginsberg to the underside of Times Square, including the addicts Bill Garver, who supported his habit by stealing coats, and Herbert

Huncke, who became, said Holmes, "a model of how to survive."[11] (Huncke's autobiography, published in 1990, was entitled *Guilty of Everything*.) Huncke was the first person Kerouac remembered using the word *beat*, a word which Kerouac thought might have come from "some midwest carnival or junk cafeteria."[12]

Initially, according to Kerouac's *Desolation Angels*, *beat* simply meant "mind-your-own-business" as in "beat it" or get out of here.[13] It meant "poor, down and out, deadbeat, on the bum, sad, sleeping in subways" ("Origins," 363). In his first novel, Kerouac described, for example, a woman "wandering 'beat' around the city in search of some other job or benefactor or 'loot' or 'gold.'"[14] Holmes added in 1952 that "more than mere weariness, ["beat"] implies the feeling of having been used, of being raw. It involves a sort of nakedness of mind, and, ultimately, of soul; a feeling of being reduced to the bedrock of consciousness. In short, it means being undramatically pushed up against the wall of oneself."[15] Kerouac later decided that the word meant "beatific" as well ("Origins," 365).

Kerouac traced the Beat Generation back to that time when "America was invested with wild self-believing individuality" ("Origins," 361). By the 1940s, however, America seemed to have little use for "wild self-believing individuality." The frontier era was long past, and the labor movement, which had portrayed the worker as defiant and independent, had become respectable and middle-class. The laborer lived nearly as well as the professional, and no one needed a Eugene Debs or a Daniel Boone any longer. The self-reliant hero had survived in the Depression songs of Woodie Guthrie and the novels of John Steinbeck and had been transformed into the GI during World War II, but young men returning from Europe and the South Pacific were not told to brave frontiers but to get an education (at government expense under the GI bill), a family, and a home.

A generation later, John F. Kennedy's New Frontier—a frontier bureaucratized, sanitized, and domesticated—would exemplify the new male ideal: a man fundamentally impersonal and unemotional. But the type was already there in the years when the Beats began to write. Men were expected to be logical, efficient, and cool-headed, organizing their lives according to their employers' needs. There was no place for the excitable, intense, and independent personality exemplified by frontier America. That older hero survived in movies and popular fiction, but essentially he was identified now as an adolescent, a stage responsible men were supposed to outgrow. A nineteenth-century hero had become a problem for social workers in the 1950s: Cooper's Natty Bumppo was now a "juvenile delinquent."

But juvenile delinquents, motorcycles, and leather jackets indicated a discontent that went much beyond adolescence. Convention and respectability had very nearly eradicated Kerouac's "America . . . invested with wild self-believing individuality," but he felt that the America he valued "suddenly began to emerge again" after World War II, when "the hipsters began to appear gliding around saying 'Crazy, man' " ("Origins," 361). The hipster adopted an ethic at odds with most Americans, and his values and view of the world soon became the Beats'. What was known in the 1950s as "beat" was essentially what had been called "hip" a decade earlier.

A few months after Burroughs, Ginsberg, and Kerouac became friends, they were brought even closer together by a murder case that led to Kerouac and Burroughs's first attempt at writing a novel. Lucien Carr had met an older man named Dave Kammerer, who fell in love with him and pursued him for several years. In the summer of 1944, Carr stabbed and killed Kammerer with a Boy Scout knife in a park near Columbia. Carr went to Kerouac and told him, and Kerouac helped him dispose of the murder weapon. They spoke to Burroughs who told Carr that he should turn himself in to the police. Two days later he did.

Burroughs and Kerouac made the Carr-Kammerer episode the subject of a jointly written novel, still unpublished, entitled "And The Hippos Were Boiled in Their Tank." (The title was taken from a radio news report of a fire at the zoo.) Aside from a few earlier sketches, this was Burroughs's first extended piece of writing, and he adopted for it the style of hard-boiled detective stories, a style which he would utilize in his first two novels, *Junky* (1953) and *Queer* (written immediately after *Junky* was completed but not published until 1985), as well as in much of his subsequent fiction. It was an ideal style with which to describe that world of moral ambiguity in which he and his friends found themselves. It was one way to deal with the hip world—a cold verbal surface beneath which, in a morass of moral ambiguities, there was always the threat of terrible violence. In *On the Road* (1957) Kerouac would develop a style which would more directly express that threat, a style which would seem intense, frantic, and driven, although two decades later when he returned to Kammerer's murder in *Vanity of Duluoz* (1968), he chose a style as cool and dispassionate as that of Burroughs.

Burroughs, who left New York in 1947, did not know Bill Cannastra, a Harvard graduate who took the cult of hip to an extreme, dancing (as reported in Ginsberg's "Howl" [1956]) "on broken wineglasses barefoot," teetering on the edge of his roof, defying violent death repeatedly, and who in 1950 was killed when he suddenly tried to climb out of the window on a subway train as it started to leave the station. He became Finistra in Kerouac's *Visions of Cody* (1972) and Agatson in Holmes's *Go* (1952). He was, in a sense, warning where the hipster's nihilism could lead (and that is how he is seen in Holmes's novel), but his life and death also exemplified the extremes to which conformist America drove the rebellious individual, and it was in that sense that he became one of the heroes, one of "the best minds," of Ginsberg's "Howl." "The first perceptions that we were separate from the official vision of history and reality, began around '45, '46, '47," Ginsberg said.[16] The official vision, the one to which the GIs returned, seemed a fantasy. The real one was a world of real horror—Kammerer's murder, Cannastra's death, and the addicts and petty thieves who passed before the windows of the Times Square cafeteria where the Beats would spend the time with Huncke or Garver. Huncke's addiction, according to Ginsberg, pointed out the difference between humanitarian matters—what the junkie need was "maintenance therapy—and official oppression" (*Composed*, 71).

Hipsters, Beats, and the True Frontier

Holmes thought his generation was "black, lost, wild and headed toward the deepest corner of the night," and yet, he insisted, "Our search is, I firmly believe, a spiritual one."[17] The Beat Generation, he wrote, was "the first generation in several centuries for which the act of faith has been an obsessive problem, quite aside from the reasons for having a particular faith or not having it. It exhibits on every side, and in a bewildering number of facets, a perfect craving to believe." (*Nothing,* 113).

In this, the role played by Neal Cassady was crucial, particularly for Ginsberg and Kerouac.[18] Cassady exemplified both hip distrust for convention and that "wild self-believing individuality" Kerouac associated with an earlier America. Cassady was a Westerner. He had grown up on the streets and in the poolhalls of Denver, and to Ginsberg and Kerouac, whose backgrounds were comparatively conventional, he exemplified freedom; he seemed to have found a way out of the darkness Holmes saw at the end of the road. "Neal had answered questions Jack couldn't answer for himself, or so Jack fancied it," Holmes said (Tytell, "Holmes," 161). Cassady could apparently do what he wished and not, like Cannastra, have to pay for it. Cassady was, of course, the impeccable driver who became Dean Moriarty in *On the Road,* and it may have been he whom Holmes had in mind when he wrote that "the giggling nihilist, eating up the highway at ninety miles an hour, and steering with his feet, . . . invites death only to outwit it. He is affirming the life within him in the only way he knows how, at the extreme" (*Nothing,* 19). In effect what Cassady did in his life, the Beats tried to do in their poetry and fiction.

Understanding the Beats

In one manner or another, all of the Beats pushed their work to extremes. Each began in the claustrophobic, oppressive world of the hipster and then moved out, testing words as Cassady tested a car to see how fast it could take a corner. There were two kinds of hipsters, "cool" and "hot," as Kerouac reported in *The Subterraneans* (1958). The former is suggested by Burroughs's restrained, neutral tone in *Junky* and *Queer*. With *Naked Lunch* (1959), however, he began writing a more extreme language, testing boundaries of diction and expression much as Ginsberg did in "Howl." Corso too learned to write with similar expressive power in such works as "Elegiac Feelings American" (1970). "Most Beat Generation artists belong to the hot school," Kerouac wrote, adding that he was originally "a hot hipster . . . who finally cooled it in Buddhist meditation" ("Origins," 363).

Although the hipster's enemy was the materialistic American, even the "cool" hipster was rarely so ascetic or austere as to cut him or herself totally off from the world. Hip culture was itself in some ways deeply commercial (or commercialized) and materialistic. Holmes saw that his generation was obsessed with spiritual questions but depended on the capitalistic economy it despised in order to spread the new ideas and values. Records, radios, cars, clothes, and books were all ways in which the hipster could express his or her ethic and identify those who shared it. The popular response to the beat writers may have in part been due to the fact that by the time "Howl" and *On the Road* were published, the ethic and attitudes they advocated had in some ways already pervaded America.

The first journal to popularize hip culture was Jay Landesman's *Neurotica,* begun in 1948. A friend who had been reading W. H. Auden's *Age of Anxiety* told Landesman, "He's got his finger on the pulse of the times. The new look is going to be the anxious look." The hipster was certainly anxious, and *Neurotica* became a major journal for hip culture. The second issue included a story by John Clellon Holmes, which Landesman thought may have been "the first piece of published fiction that utilized the language of the hipster."[19] *Neurotica* dealt with much more than hip culture, and although some of its contributors, such as Chandler Brossard, rejected the hip world, Landesman's journal was important in preparing readers for the sort of literature they were soon to get from Kerouac, Ginsberg, and Holmes.

Although widely circulated, *Neurotica* was read by a relatively small, but sophisticated, group of Americans. Anyone could get something of the hip style, however, simply by going to the movies, where the hipster's mannerisms were incorporated into the acting styles of Marlon Brando, Paul Newman, Montgomery Clift, and James Dean. Hipster culture was the subject of such popular films as *Young Man with a Horn* (1950) starring Kirk Douglas, *The Man with the Golden Arm* (1956) featuring Frank Sinatra, and *All the Fine Young Cannibals* (1959) with Robert Wagner. *Film noir* also incorporated the hipster's paranoid view of civilization.

One could also find hip culture and attitudes by listening to Symphony Sid's all-night jazz program on the radio in New York or the weekly broadcasts from Manhattan's Birdland. This kind of jazz, bepob or just bop, as it was called, would have a major influence on rhythms in Corso's, Ginsberg's, and particularly Kerouac's work. Bop arose in the early 1940s, although its great popularity did not arrive until the middle of the decade. In 1942, as part of an action against licensing agencies, the musicians' union banned its members from making recordings. The ban lasted more than two years during which bop musicians were able to go their own way without having to acquiesce to the public's taste. Before 1942, jazz was determined very much by the big bands, which, because of their size, left little room for spontaneity or improvisation. The arranger and the band's leader (sometimes the same person) dominated the music. But bop was performed by small groups in which improvisation was encouraged. This music, with its emphasis on the individual, was quintessentially hip, and such record companies as Blue Note and Contemporary made the music of Charlie Parker, Dizzy Gillespie, and other bop musicians widely available.[20]

Beat poetry and fiction were rooted in hip culture, but they also drew from literary traditions which encouraged personal and spontaneous styles. Rimbaud and Whitman were among their principal forerunners. Among twentieth-century predecessors, Ginsberg pointed specifically to French Surrealists and Gertrude Stein (*Composed,* 88). Stein was especially important, for both her fiction and poetry were major contributions to expressionist aesthetics, and the Beats were strongly indebted to the expressionist tradition.

The word *expressionism,* as R. S. Furness wrote, "has to cover so many disparate cultural manifestations as to be virtually meaningless," yet it is conventionally identified with "self-expression, creativity, ecstatic fervour and a ruthless denial of tradition." Expressionism implies the discovery of meaning which no objective analysis or consensus can reach and which is found within the self rather than through a study of society or history. Expressionist writing is, although subjective, not solipsistic (or so the writer claims), for it achieves a level of experience and understanding that is not merely personal but common, or at least potentially common, to all readers. According to Henry Miller, the artist "recreates [the universe] out of his own experience and understanding of life."[21]

Expressionism in American literature has its roots in Ralph Waldo Emerson, who asserted in his essay "The Poet" that "the Universe is the externization of the soul," but the great expressionist poet was Walt Whitman, who in one of the finer humorous and arrogant moments in *Song of Myself* identified the voice of his poem as "Walt Whitman, a kosmos, of Manhattan the son." He meant that literally, of course: both a man in the city and "a kosmos." "In all people I see myself," he said in another comic but at the same time utterly serious moment, "none more and not one a barleycorn less."

American expressionism as it developed from Whitman should be distinguished from German Expressionism, which is a related but quite separate movement, and the romantic search for transcendent moments when the division between the self and the universe was seemingly eclipsed.[22] For the romantic, those sublime moments occurred at best sporadically; there were discrete occasions of sudden illumination. For the American expressionist, however, the most personal, even ordinary occasion had its universal character. As Michael McClure wrote, "I did not fear obscurity in my poetry because I had come to believe that the way to the universal was by means of the most intensely personal. I believed that what we truly share with others lies in the deepest, most personal, even physiological core—and not in the outer social world of speech that is used for grooming and transactions."[23]

The expressionist has a particular mission when realism and materialism are dominant. For the realist, language is at best transparent, designating a reality separate from itself, and the author is in the extreme instance, therefore, not visible in the work. Expressionist writing can be personal and autobiographical, but it does not have to be. It may draw on personal experience, may indeed be deeply confessional, but it has the potential to do much more than celebrate the private self. Perhaps few expressionists would make as large a claim as Whitman's—"In all people I see myself"—but the expressionist aesthetic gave William Saroyan, for example, permission to speak for Armenian-Americans and William Faulkner permission to speak for the South.

Gertrude Stein, in a review of Sherwood Anderson's *A Story Teller's Story,* pointed out that what he did in his work was "express life" rather than document or "embroider" it.[24] He was, that is, not a writer in those realistic and naturalistic traditions with which he had often been (and occasionally still is) mistakenly associated. Anderson had listened to his father tell stories and found that his father's success depended on the manner of telling rather than on matters of character and plot. The story's real subject, in other words, was the narrator. Taking that as a starting point, Anderson's usual approach was to locate an episode and a narrator, bring them together, and let the story go wherever the occasion indicated—an intuitive rather than a traditional or formalist approach. His stories are spoken narratives depending directly on the rhythms of spoken English for their effects, much as Mark Twain's had been.

Anderson's disciples in the 1920s and 1930s included William Faulkner, Ernest Hemingway, Thomas Wolfe, and William Saroyan. Kerouac cited the last three as major influences on his work, and one of his early novels, *Pic* (not published until 1971 although written in 1951), was obviously inspired by Faulkner. At first Kerouac tried to imitate surface elements of other expressionists. He wrote stories, as he put it in *Vanity of Duluoz*, "in the Saroyan-Hemingway-Wolfe style" and modeled the prose in *The Town and the City* on Thomas Wolfe's. But the true expressionist cannot merely imitate or borrow surface characteristics from other works. The writer must find a language and a rhythm which allows him or her to speak directly from the self. The book in which Kerouac first did that was *On the Road*, the principal draft of which was written in three weeks and so required a direct, improvisatory style: there was no time to imitate.

According to Allen Ginsberg, there is "a tradition of prose in America, including Thomas Wolfe and going through Kerouac, which is personal, in which the prose sentence is completely personal, comes from the writer's own person—his person defined as his body, his breathing rhythm, his actual talk."[25] This was what Kerouac discovered in writing *On the Road*, perfected in *Visions of Cody*, and named "spontaneous prose."

Ginsberg spoke of "a tradition of prose," but expressionism is of equal significance in American poetry in general and beat poetry in particular. The principal source is certainly Whitman, but D. H. Lawrence, particularly in *Birds, Beasts and Flowers* (1923), may have had greater influence on Kenneth Rexroth and William Everson, among other American poets in the generation immediately preceding the Beats. Other essential influences include Rimbaud, Stein, and the Surrealists.

Holmes noted that at the end of World War II, "man was seen as a victim, either of toilet training [Freud] or his place in society [Marx], but he was determined from the outside. That conception of man we all found, quite independently because we all have different backgrounds, to be increasingly inadequate" (Tytell, "Holmes," 165). Expressionism gave the Beats an aesthetic that avoided the rationalism of both Freudians and Marxists. There were also quasi-religious implications as Ginsberg recognized when he asserted that "poetry is the record of individual insights into the secret soul of the individual—and, because all individuals are One in the eyes of their Creator, into the soul of the World."[26]

By the time the Beats appeared, expressionist writing (unless it was a *cause célèbre* like Miller's *Tropic of Cancer*) seldom received a sympathetic hearing in established literary journals or in the universities. Saroyan had been dismissed, Wolfe was considered a writer for adolescents, and Lionel Trilling, rereading Anderson's works, found that he liked them "even less" than he remembered. R. P. Blackmur, preferring "objective" to "expressive" form, felt that the latter was a "heresy" and a "plague."[27]

Under these circumstances, it is not surprising that the conservative critic Norman Podhoretz could dismiss Kerouac's "conception of feeling [as] one that only a solipsist could believe in'' and could argue that he and Ginsberg shared with juvenile delinquents a "resentment against normal feeling and the attempt to cope with the world through intelligence.'' Nor is it surprising that the formalist poet John Ciardi could insist that beat writing had "been systematically vitiated by [the] insistence on the holiness of the impromptu and by the urge to play the lunatic.'' Ciardi concluded that Kerouac was "basically a high school athlete who went from Lowell, Massachusetts, to Skid Row, losing his eraser en route.''[28]

The first friendly attempts to discuss the Beats came from writers rather than from professional or academic critics.[29] The first sympathetic work was Holmes's novel *Go* (1952), in which the term *Beat Generation,* which Kerouac had proposed in 1948, appeared in print for the first time. *Go* is not an expressionistic work, and Holmes was critical about much that he and his friends did (his portrait of a misogynistic Cassady is particularly unattractive). In both style and sensibility, *Go* is the work of an outsider—a man who wanted to be hip but who, as the novel reveals, was too constrained and conservative. He was, however, a close observer and knew Ginsberg, Kerouac, Cannastra, Ansen, Cassady, and other members of the early beat group very well. *Go* is in effect a history of their lives from 1948 to 1950. As Holmes reported in his introduction to a 1980 reprint, the novel is "almost literal truth,'' even reporting "whole conversations . . . verbatim.''[30]

The principal figures in the novel are Ginsberg (David Stofsky), Kerouac (Gene Pasternak), Cassady (Hart Kennedy), Huncke (Albert Ancke), Cannastra (Agatson), and Holmes (Paul Hobbes). As the name Hobbes suggests,

Holmes portrayed himself as crippled or "hobbled" by the world and his own values, yet he does share with Stofsky and Pasternak a discontent bordering on desperation and a sense that traditional values have become pointless. To be hip or "beat" is one way to respond, but Hobbes has to will himself to act that way, while it is natural to others.

Hobbes is self-conscious in a way Pasternak and Stofsky are not and as a result does not share "their thirsty avidity for raw experience, their pragmatic quest for the unusual, the 'real,' the crazy" (*Go*, 35). Stofsky decides that he "wants a break-through into the world of feeling" and has "decided to believe in God." "All systems," he says, "are just mirrors, mirrors. You look into them and see only your self, with the world as the dim background" (*Go*, 65). In fact, Hobbes's marriage is a mirror of his own narrow ethics and imagination, but he never quite realizes that.

"Everyone I know," says Pasternak, "is kind of furtive, kind of beat. . . . And it's happening all over the country, to everyone; a sort of revolution of the soul . . . " (*Go*, 36). For Holmes, as for Kerouac, this new generation was typified by Neal Cassady (Hart Kennedy). Although Kennedy is far more callous than Kerouac's Cody Pomeray, Holmes still saw Cassady as gifted with great energy and independence and, therefore, able to resist pressures to conform. Agatson has equally great energy and can be "possessed by a demon of fantastic anarchy" (*Go*, 269), but his death leads Hobbes to realize how desperate life has become for his circle of friends. Trapped in his pointless marriage, he has at the end of the book "a vision of unending lovelessness" and believes that this same vision "must have entered [Agatson] like a germ and corrupted his heart and mind.'' A person in that circumstance would lose hope, be ''outraged, violated, raped in his soul,'' and be left in the end with ''the consuming desire to jeer, spit, curse, smash, destroy'' (*Go*, 310).

Holmes said of his generation that ''their own lust for freedom, and the ability to live at a pace that kills, (to which war had adjusted them), led to black markets, bebop, narcotics, sexual promiscuity, hucksterism and Jean-Paul Sartre. The beatness set in later'' (*Nothing*, 111). Here, as in *Go*, Holmes was speaking as a traditional, perhaps even Victorian, moralist, believing that America, having lost its values, could cure its discontents only by going faster—a solution that in its obvious pointlessness only exposed further the underlying desperation. To stop running would be to face the ''vision of unending lovelessness'' and the solitude it implied. Since Holmes's generation, as he saw it, had no fundamental values, it had no adequate cure for the predicament in which it was caught. Melville, of course, had made similar observations. Only by keeping busy and involved with his work could the narrator of *Bartleby the Scrivener* prevent himself from having to confront the fact that in his success he was as isolated as Bartleby.

For Holmes, Bartleby, and Melville's narrator, solitude and ''unending lovelessness'' are the penalties for ''wild self-believing individuality.'' For Holmes the collapse of Hobbes's marriage was a terrible thing, but that Holmes should have felt that way is a measure of how conservative a moralist he was. American heroes from Natty Bumppo to Huck Finn to Nick Adams fled exactly what Holmes seeks. The price for freedom (Ishmael's, Hester Prynne's, Huck Finn's, Thoreau's, Pasternak's,

Kennedy's, Agatson's) may be "unending lovelessness," but that never deterred heroes in American myth and literature.

Insisting, in McClure's words, that "the way to the universal was by means of the most intensely personal," expressionism provided a solution to "unending loveless-ness." Holmes was a fairly conventional writer and not an expressionist, but other Beats found in the expressionist aesthetic an escape from the solitude that cursed Agatson. "Whitman all along had said that private consciousness *is* public consciousness," wrote Ginsberg (*Composed*, 72).

Although the deterioration of Hobbes's marriage is the central tragedy in *Go,* none of the principal characters aside from Hobbes and his wife is affected by it. Holmes is not suggesting merely that Hobbes's tragedy is a private matter; he is suggesting that marriage itself and traditional relationships between men and women have no place in the new world he is describing.

Marriage in fact had little significance in the beat world. Ginsberg in his journal in 1954 recorded a dream in which he received a letter from Holmes saying, "The social organization which is most true of itself to the artist is the boy gang," to which Ginsberg himself added, "not soci-ety's perfum'd marriage."[31]

Women have little place in most beat writings. There are few women in Ginsberg's work outside of such poems as "Kaddish" and "White Shroud," which concern his mother and other women in his family. Corso's "Mar-riage" is one of two well known mid-century poems attack-ing its subject, and various early poems by him involve grotesque images of women, particularly mothers. In *Visions of Cody* Kerouac wrote, "As far as young women are concerned I can't look at them unless I tear off their clothes one by one."[32]

Burroughs's fiction can be severely misogynistic, but as Jennie Skerl has noted, "his attacks upon women in general are attacks upon women's roles within a certain social structure."[33] In this he followed that conspicuous American literary tradition which characterizes men as renegades and advocates of freedom and women as defenders of decorum, domesticity, and the status quo. It is the distinction between Becky Thatcher and Huck Finn in which the woman is (unless a comic figure) the antithesis of Kerouac's "wild self-believing individuality." Not surprisingly Burroughs called the family a "formula" that had to be dissolved. " 'Women,' " he said, quoting a character in Conrad's *Victory*, " 'are a perfect curse.' "[34]

"I realize I am widely perceived as a misogynist," Burroughs wrote in an essay entitled "Women: A Biological Mistake?" But in fact, he continued, he would suggest androgyny, "the sexes fusing into an organism," as "the next step" in evolutionary development. The real villain he remarked in an interview, is romantic love: "love is a fraud perpetrated by the female sex." Sexual relations between men do not involve "love, but rather what we might call *recognition*."[35] What Burroughs would choose, as his novels repeatedly make clear, is sexuality unencumbered by illusions or sentiment—and that was not the way relations between men and women were conceived when the Beats began to write.

All that changed radically in the 1960s and 1970s, of course, and "the boy gang" very quickly became anachronistic. The hipster values the Beats promoted did not disappear, however. The Beats, as Gregory Stephenson wrote, were concerned with "knowledge of the Self, and the discovery or recovery of a true mode of perception"— objectives obviously equally important to feminists.[36] Younger women writers learned much from Burroughs, Corso, Ginsberg, and Kerouac, and if the second generation of the Beats included such important male writers as Ed Sanders, Clark Coolidge, and Sam Shepard, it also included many highly regarded women poets such as Diane di Prima, Anne Waldman, and Alice Notley as well as Patti Smith, Laurie Anderson, and other popular singers and performers.

Notes

1. Paul O'Neil, "The Only Rebellion Around," *Life* 47 (30 November 1959): 115.
2. Donald Allen, ed., *Off the Wall: Interviews with Philip Whalen* (Bolinas, CA: Four Seasons, 1978) 62.
3. Parkinson identifies the specifically local roots of the San Francisco Renaissance in "Phenomenon or Generation," *A Casebook on the Beat* (New York: Crowell, 1961) 276–90.
4. Inger Thorup Lauridsen and Per Dalgard, *The Beat Generation and the Russian New Wave* (Ann Arbor: Ardis, 1990) 67–68; James McKenzie, "Moving the World an Inch" (interview with Gary Snyder), *The Beat Vision,* ed. Arthur and Kit Knight (New York: Paragon, 1987) 2; Lauridsen and Dalgard, 135.
5. Lauridsen and Dalgard, 115.
6. Daniel Odier, *The Job: Interviews with William S. Burroughs* (New York: Grove, 1974) 43.

7. Michael Andre, "An Interview with Gregory Corso," *Unmuzzled Ox* 22 (Winter 1981): 123.

8. He was born in 1914; Kerouac was born in 1922, Ginsberg in 1926, Corso in 1930.

9. Norman Mailer, "The White Negro," *Advertisements for Myself* (New York: Putnam's, 1959) 339.

10. Mailer, 339. Gerald Nicosia discusses differences between Mailer's view of the hipster and Kerouac's in *Memory Babe: A Critical Biography of Jack Kerouac* (New York: Grove, 1983) 206.

11. John Tytell, "An Interview with John Clellon Holmes," *Kerouac and the Beats,* ed. Arthur and Kit Knight (New York: Paragon, 1988), 166. Subsequent references are given parenthetically in the text.

12. Jack Kerouac, "The Origins of the Beat Generation," *On the Road: Text and Criticism,* ed. Scott Donaldson (New York: Viking, 1979), 362. Subsequent references are given parenthetically in the text.

13. Jack Kerouac, *Desolation Angels* (New York: Coward-McCann, 1965) 319.

14. Jack Kerouac, *The Town and the City* (New York: Harcourt, Brace, 1950) 451.

15. John Clellon Holmes, "This Is the Beat Generation," *Nothing More to Declare* (New York: Dutton, 1967) 110. The article originally appeared in 1952. Subsequent references are given parenthetically in the text.

16. Allen Ginsberg, *Composed on the Tongue* (Bolinas, CA: Grey Fox, 1980) 71. Subsequent references are given parenthetically in the text.

17. John Clellon Holmes, "Crazy Days, Numinous Nights: 1948–1950," *The Beat Vision,* ed. Arthur and Kit Knight, 86.

18. The only biography of Cassady to date is William Plummer's *The Holy Goof* (Englewood Cliffs, NJ: Prentice-Hall, 1981). Cassady's published writings are collected in *The First Third* (San Francisco: City Lights, 1971).

19. Jay Landesman, *Rebel Without Applause* (New York: Paragon, 1990) 45, 55.

20. On connections between bop, on the one hand, and hipsters and the Beats, on the other, see Roy Carr, Brian Case, and Fred Dellar, *The Hip: Hipsters, Jazz and the Beat Generation* (London: Faber and Faber, 1986).

21. R. S. Furness, *Expressionism* (London: Methuen, 1973) 1, 14; Henry Miller, "An Open Letter to Surrealists Everywhere," *The Cosmological Eye* (New York: New Directions, 1939) 193.

22. Sherrill E. Grace traces parallels between German Expressionism and works by Canadian writers and such American writers as Eugene

Understanding the Beats

O'Neill in *Regression and Apocalypse: Studies in North American Literary Expressionism* (Toronto: University of Toronto Press, 1989). American expressionists like Sherwood Anderson, Henry Miller, Thomas Wolfe, and William Saroyan derived their aesthetics ultimately, however, from Whitman rather than from German writers such as Gottfried Benn, Alfred Döblin, and Ernst Toller.

23. Michael McClure, *Scratching the Beat Surface* (San Francisco: North Point, 1982) 26.

24. Gertrude Stein, Review of *A Story Teller's Story,* in *Sherwood Anderson: A Collection of Critical Essays,* ed. Walter B. Rideout (Englewood Cliffs, NJ: Prentice-Hall, 1974) 86.

25. Allen Ginsberg, *Allen Verbatim: Lectures on Poetry, Politics, Consciousness,* ed. Gordon Ball (New York: McGraw-Hill, 1974) 153.

26. Allen Ginsberg, "Poetry, Violence, and the Trembling Lambs," *The Poetics of the New American Poetry,* ed. Donald Allen and Warren Tallman (New York: Grove, 1973) 331.

27. Lionel Trilling, "Sherwood Anderson," *The Liberal Imagination* (Garden City, NY: Anchor Books, 1953) 21; R. P. Blackmur, *The Expense of Greatness* (New York: Arrow Editions, 1940) 190; *The Double Agent* (New York: Arrow Editions), 105.

28. Norman Podhoretz, "The Know-Nothing Bohemians," *On the Road: Text and Criticism,* ed. Donaldson, 353, 355; John Ciardi, "Epitaph for the Dead Beats," *Dialogue with an Audience* (Philadelphia: Lippincott, 1963) 304.

29. The first major critical book by an academic was *Casebook on the Beat* (1961), Thomas Parkinson's collection of works by and about the Beats, but Parkinson was himself a respected poet, associated early in his career with Jack Spicer, William Everson, Robert Duncan, and Kenneth Rexroth.

30. John Clellon Holmes, *Go* (New York: New American Library, 1980) xvii–xviii. Subsequent references are given parenthetically in the text.

31. Allen Ginsberg, *Journals: Early Fifties Early Sixties* (New York: Grove, 1977) 80. This reference came to my attention through Catharine R. Stimpson, "The Beat Generation and the Trials of Homosexual Liberation," *Salamagundi* 58/59 (Fall/Winter 1982–83): 373–92.

32. Corso's "Marriage" is discussed in chapter four. The other poem, also entitled "Marriage," is by Marianne Moore; Jack Kerouac, *Visions of Cody* (New York: McGraw-Hill, 1972) 23.

33. Jennie Skerl, *William S. Burroughs* (Boston: Twayne, 1985) 4.

34. Odier, *The Job,* 42, 110.

Hipsters, Beats, and the True Frontier

35. William S. Burroughs, ''Women: A Biological Mistake?'' *The Adding Machine* (New York: Seaver, 1986) 126; Odier, *The Job*, 112.

36. Gregory Stephenson, ''The 'Spiritual Optics' of Lawrence Fer-linghetti,'' in *Beat Indeed!*, ed. Rudi Horemans (Antwerp: EXA, 1985) 117.

CHAPTER TWO

Kerouac

It's generally construed that Jack underwent some sort of a change and became more conservative. But he was always conservative. Those ideas never changed. He was always the same. It was sort of a double-think. In one way he was a Buddhist with this expansionistic viewpoint, and on the other hand he always had the most conservative political opinions. He was an Eisenhower man and he believed in the old-fashioned virtues.

—William S. Burroughs,
quoted by Barry Gifford and Lawrence Lee in
Jack's Book: An Oral Biography of Jack Kerouac

Jean-Louis (Jack) Kerouac was born to French-Canadian parents on 12 March 1922 in Lowell, a factory town in northeastern Massachusetts. When Kerouac was four, his brother Gerard died. Although Gerard was only nine, he had seemed a saint to his relatives and friends. "The whole reason why I ever wrote at all . . . ," Kerouac said, was "because of Gerard, the idealism, Gerard the religious hero."[1] Memories of his brother's illness and sufferings never left Kerouac, and his work is marked by a sense that life is sacred but tenuous and painful.

Kerouac's mother, Gabrielle, whom he called Mémère, offered whatever comfort she could. His father, he wrote, "told me to take care of my mother on his deathbed."[2] She became the only woman to whom he could turn, and his deepest affection was reserved for her. In *Desolation Angels* (1965), he used her as the model for Duluoz's mother, the only solace for his sufferings. Kerouac's books rarely suggest that anything except a maternal relationship could be permanently satisfactory between men and women.

In all of his major work Kerouac seeks ways to transcend or ameliorate suffering. Emerson and Thoreau had lived only a few miles from Lowell, and Kerouac, before he left for college, considered living as Thoreau had at Walden. New England transcendentalism certainly marked Kerouac, but his French-Catholic background was stronger. If there were moments of grace when he seemed to have overcome the suffering of this world, he was soon brought back to where he had been. There are few happy endings in Kerouac.

Kerouac's father ran a successful printing business, but in 1936 it was destroyed in a flood, and from then until his death, Leo Kerouac never regained his independence. That failure and his final anguish (Kerouac cared for him in 1946 as he died of cancer) surely reinforced convictions that ultimately life is suffering.

Kerouac was a good athlete at Lowell High School and, after a year at the Horace Mann School in New York City, entered Columbia in 1940 on a football scholarship. His father wanted him to go to Boston College, which, like Columbia, had recruited him as a football player. His father's employer, who did the printing for Boston College, also thought that should be the choice. Kerouac believed that his father lost his job because the Boston offer was turned down. Whether or not that was true (and there is apparently nothing except Kerouac's claim to substantiate it) is beside the point. As long as he believed it was so, he felt guilty for what he believed he had done to his father.

Kerouac never became the football player Columbia wanted. In his freshman year he broke his leg shortly after the season began, and in 1941 he left both the team and the college at the beginning of the school year. The following spring he joined the merchant marine and served until October, then returned to Columbia and the football team but soon left again. He joined the navy, but one day when he decided to read rather than follow orders, he was put under psychiatric care and eventually honorably discharged. Again he served in the merchant marine and then traveled around the country. By the spring of 1944 he was back in New York living near Columbia with Edie Parker, an art student whom he had known since 1942.

Parker introduced him to her friend Lucien Carr, who in turn introduced him to Allen Ginsberg and Dave Kammerer. Carr confided in Kerouac after Kammerer's murder, and when Carr was arrested, Kerouac was also arrested and held as a material witness. He and Parker were married while he was in jail. They then went to Michigan and lived briefly with her parents, but in October, he returned to New York and soon reestablished his friendship with Ginsberg and Burroughs. The marriage was soon annulled.

By any conventional standard, Kerouac was, like his father, a failure, but unlike his father, it seemed as if he had chosen to fail—as if he had done what he could not to be the respectable, successful son his parents wanted. Men like Huncke and Garver survived on the fringes of American life, yet they did survive while Leo Kerouac suffered one defeat after another and became increasingly bitter.

According to John Clellon Holmes, "at first Jack wanted to be like his father. He started being nostalgic about life in Lowell when he was seventeen, perhaps even earlier. But he never felt part of it. He was like Rimbaud." (Tytell, "Holmes," 161). There is a great tension in Kerouac's work between his father's values, which were conservative and traditional, and the hipster values and point of view shared with Burroughs, Ginsberg, and other friends in New York. But his father's stable world had vanished in 1936. The values remained, but the economic and social systems which had supported them were gone. Some of Kerouac's new friends were "beat"—worn, defeated—but having accepted that, they found resilience and humor. While Leo Kerouac repeatedly failed economically and spiritually, those who admitted they were outsiders survived.

Kerouac was caught between two incompatible possibilities, the world of his parents and the world of his friends, and he made that dilemma the subject of his first novel, *The Town and the City.* He worked on the novel while caring for his father during the final illness, but most of the work was done after Leo's death. The book was finished in 1948 and published two years later. *The Town and the City,* although it is an apprentice novel, gives an effective picture of America during that period when the traditional culture of small towns and Emersonian self-reliance was being overpowered by the commercial, aggressive, impersonal culture of the cities. The novel provides as well an introduction to Kerouac's major concerns in his fiction. He had not yet discovered a style characteristically his own, but his central interests were already set.

The Town and the City is concerned with the loss of Leo Kerouac's world. George Martin, whom Kerouac modeled on his father, has five sons and three daughters and lives in one of the best houses in Galloway, a New England town based on Lowell. Martin has been a dutiful husband and father, but he is ruined in business by trusted associates. He is in a sense brought down by his failure to understand that America is no longer the just and equitable place he thinks it is and that it is no longer enough simply to be good and self-reliant in order to survive.

The Town and the City deals with the simple economic revelation of the Depression era, in which the first part of the book is set: the discovery that the economic system was inherently unjust and not, as generations of laissez-faire economists had argued, fundamentally equitable and moral. That, of course, was what leftist idealogues had always argued, but to fundamentally conservative people like the Kerouacs, the failure of the economic system was traumatic. All of Kerouac's work may in fact be read as an effort to preserve the libertarian ideal of self-reliance in a civilization where personal success was no longer testimony of moral worth.

Having lost his business, George Martin has to work for other men, and since he now has less money, he must sell his house and move his family into a tenement. He then loses his job because of sickness but eventually finds work in New York. He is depressed and angered by the city's cold and mercenary nature. Like Kerouac's father, he suffers from cancer, and the book ends with his death and funeral.

Kerouac transforms the conventional theme that the small town is good and the city is impersonal and corrupt into an elegy for his father. There is great poignance in

George Martin's defeat. He is a man who in another age would have been a respected citizen and father, but he has been ruined by circumstances beyond his control and then deserted by his children, who realize that the new age has no place for his values and, therefore, set out to find new ways to survive. He cannot approve of their lives and is embittered.

Martin's sons, particularly Joe, Peter, and Francis, suggest different ways Kerouac saw himself.[3] Joe, the oldest, is the son most like his father and may indicate the kind of man Kerouac might have been if he never left Lowell. In some ways Joe, as Warren French has indicated, is also reminiscent of Neal Cassady, whom Kerouac met while he was writing the novel. Joe's ambition is to get a motorcycle "so that he [can] hurl himself plummeting and roaring along to anywhere." He wishes he had lived in the pioneer era, "when America was America."[4] At the end of the book, he buys a farm as his father had always wanted to do. Joe is free because he does not have his father's responsibilities, but one wonders what will happen to his life after he has settled into his new obligations.

The young Francis is melancholy and bitter, wanting to get away from his home and "extricate myself from all this forever" (*TC*, 189). He meets a sophisticated and rather prissy intellectual named Wilfred Engels, who argues that the Great Depression was a good thing as it permitted certain necessary changes. Human suffering is merely the necessary cost; what matters to Engels are abstract, theoretical questions. Francis retreats into books and ideas and, at the end of the novel, is planning to go to Paris and study at the Sorbonne.

Arguing that Francis and Peter represent a fundamental split in Kerouac and preferring the side identified as Francis, Warren French asks "what would have happened had Francis prevailed and launched Kerouac on a career that would have paralleled James Joyce's or Henry Miller's search for intellectual fulfillment in expatriation."[5] However, Kerouac's achievement depended on avoiding the kind of "intellectual fulfillment" and abstract reasoning respected by Francis, and it can hardly be said that Miller (who admired Kerouac) was an intellectual, at least of Francis's sort. The arid academic abstractions in which Francis lives repelled both Miller and Kerouac. For Kerouac, Francis's tragedy is greater than his father's.

Francis's idol Wilfred Engels is appropriately named. According to Ginsberg, Kerouac was "overtly communistic for several years, from '39 to '41, '42" (*Composed*, 74), but by the time *The Town and the City* was written, he had little faith in leftist ideologies. The solutions which Marxists had proposed to heal the traumas of the Depression were not his. The historical Engels may have once seemed to Kerouac a thinker whose ideas showed the way out of economic injustice, but the Engels in *The Town and the City* is a sardonic ideologue and false prophet.

The third brother, Peter, is the one most like the author at the time he wrote the book. Peter, like Kerouac, was a football star who came home from college, "put on his old blue denims, went swimming in the brook in the pine woods with his chums, loafed around reading Jack London and Walt Whitman" (*TC*, 131). He seems at first more conventional than Joe and Francis but he proves to be a greater rebel, for Joe's wanderings only lead back home, and Francis is too caustic and austere to move far beyond his own ideas and regrets. Peter, however, is a man of intense emotions, ranging from the fear of defeat he experiences as a football hero to the anger and affection he feels toward his father. His complex emotional nature allows him to experience and understand things others do not. He "literally stare[s] into the abyss" and learns what "could not be learned in any school" (*TC*, 260). Francis, feeling as an adolescent and young man that he is not understood, turns contemptuously on the world, but Peter feels loneliness, grief, and loss. He is the true wanderer, the Ishmael, who at the end of the novel puts on his black leather jacket and starts hitchhiking with no certain destination. He is the prototype for Jack Duluoz, Ray Smith, and Sal Paradise—other characters Kerouac modeled on himself.

Peter's life follows a pattern familiar in American literature—the story of the young man who leaves the small town to confront the great world—but with an important difference: the town left behind is confining and oppressive. Sherwood Anderson's *Winesburg, Ohio* (1919), for example, presents a village of grotesques, men and women warped by narrow moral expectations, and the main character, George Willard, makes the right choice in leaving it. The same is true for Eugene Gant in Thomas Wolfe's *Look Homeward, Angel,* published in 1929. Small-town America was disappearing from Kerouac's world, however, and it was possible to view it with a nostalgia an earlier generation did not feel. In *The Town and the City,* the Martins are forced to leave Galloway for economic reasons, and that is the source of the book's tragedy.

In New York, Peter is surrounded with people whom Kerouac based on his friends: Leon Levinsky (Ginsberg), Kenneth Wood (Carr), Will Dennison (Burroughs), Mary

Dennison (Burroughs's common-law wife, Joan Vollmer), Junkey (Huncke), Judie Smith (Edie Parker), and Waldo Meister (David Kammerer), among others. Kammerer's murder does not enter into the book (Meister commits suicide), but his homosexual obsession with Carr is clearly reflected, and there are graphic descriptions of the world of drugs and sexual deviance associated with Times Square. Essentially this setting is the hipster world, and *The Town and the City* is among the first novels to describe it.

Peter's friends not only understand the new urban America which has replaced small towns like Galloway but also have found ways to survive it. Levinsky says that "virus X" has invaded American life, and "all character-structures based on tradition and uprightness and so-called morality will slowly rot away." It's "the great molecular comedown," he says; it is "like the plague, only this time it will ruin everything" (*TC*, 370–71). Kerouac is quoting here from an essay Ginsberg wrote, but the ideas are derived from the German thinker Oswald Spengler, whom both men had been reading in a copy of *The Decline of the West* given to them by Burroughs.

Spengler and "the great molecular comedown" help to explain the failure of George Martin's world. Levinsky calls the collapse "a kind of universal cancer" (*TC*, 370–71), and it is literally cancer that kills Peter's father. Levinsky and George Martin both know that America is being destroyed: "Something *evil* and awful has happened," George Martin says, "there's nothing but unhappiness everywhere" (*TC*, 423). But in spite of what his father and Levinsky believe and in spite of what he has seen himself, Peter retains some of his earlier idealism and concludes, somewhat sentimentally, that "children and fathers should have a notion in their souls that there must be a way, an authority, a great knowledge, a vision, a view of life, a proper manner, an order in all the disorder and sadness of the world—that alone must be God in men" (*TC*, 424). Sentimental as this passage is, it can be seen as expressing an important assumption underlying Kerouac's fiction, in which he would repeatedly search for "a way, an authority, a great knowledge" and would find it by returning in the end to Leo Kerouac's values and religion.

The principal shortcomings in *The Town and the City* are persistent sentimentality and nostalgia, which prevent the author from confronting and trying to understand the economic and social changes that have destroyed the Martin family. In this at least, it is unfortunate that Peter (and Kerouac) could not have been, like Francis, ironic and detached.

These shortcomings are found as well in the works of writers, particularly Thomas Wolfe and William Saroyan, whose fiction Kerouac followed in creating *The Town and the City*. Kerouac's style here, is developed principally from Wolfe, and the Martins are idealized much as are the Macauleys in Saroyan's *The Human Comedy* (1943). Galloway resembles the all-American town of Ithaca in Saroyan's novel, and when Kerouac says that "Peter was seized with a tremendous mournfulness of heart" or that he realizes "what a strange sad adventure life might get to be," he echoes Saroyan and Wolfe (*TC*, 259, 127). Peter might also be compared to Saroyan's daring young man on the flying trapeze, indifferent to his fate and, therefore, free while others are cautious and prudent.

In *The Town and the City,* Kerouac was still imitating superficial mannerisms and attitudes—Saroyan's sweetness and Wolfe's broadly romantic sentences. Kerouac tried to write like his predecessors but achieved instead a pastiche of stylistic gestures and attitudes which did not cohere in a unified sensibility and vision. The prose rhythms are generally drawn from Wolfe and move in large "symphonic" gestures.[6] At the end of the book, for example, Peter is "on the road again, traveling the continent westward, going off to further and further years, alone by the waters of life, alone, looking towards the lights of the river's cape, towards tapers burning warmly in the towns, looking down along the shore in remembrance of the dearness of his father and of all life" (*TC,* 498–99). In this "symphonic" style, "going west" becomes "traveling the continent westward." The rhythm and tone are obviously central to the writing, but they seem more a homage to Wolfe than the author's own.

Kerouac's work after *The Town and the City* is divided chronologically into three periods: the early books, beginning with *On the Road,* in which he developed his "spontaneous prose"; a middle period, in which Buddhist works such as *The Scripture of the Golden Eternity* (1960) and *Visions of Gerard* were written; and a final period, in which his Buddhist faith and his hope that suffering could be overcome are diminished or lost.

Those who know Kerouac's writing may prefer such later works as *Visions of Cody,* "October in the Railroad Earth," *Mexico City Blues, Desolation Angels,* and especially *Big Sur,* but *On the Road* (written in 1951, published

in 1957) is the book which made him famous, and it is still
the book for which he is best known. He had been working
on it for two and a half years before he began the version
eventually published. In the spring of 1951, high on ben-
zedrine and typing a hundred words a minute, he wrote that
version on one long roll of paper in three weeks. Viking re-
portedly required extensive revisions, but as Kerouac told
Holmes, they did not get what they wanted. The published
book may be, aside from being organized into paragraphs,
very much what was typed out in 1951.[7]

Although it was done, Kerouac said, in "the spontaneous style," it was not written according to the aesthetic
of "spontaneous prose," which he did not develop until
several months after the novel was finished. The way Kerouac worked forced him to devise a style antithetical to the
graceful, symphonic sentences in *The Town and the City*
and, in Ginsberg's words, "discover the rhythm of the
mind at work at high speed in prose."[8] The need to set the
book down on paper as fast as he could gave his language
an urgency that corresponds to the urgency of the story itself. The pressure of writing and the pressure of the story
intersect, and the prose is not merely about a series of episodes but suggests directly in the rush of language the
characters' excitement and intensity.

Although Kerouac told Ted Berrigan that "the idea for
the spontaneous style of *On the Road* [came] from seeing
how good old Neal Cassady wrote his letters to me, all first
person, fast, mad, confessional, completely serious, all detailed," he had earlier told Cassady that he had been em-
ulating Burroughs's Dashiell Hammett style.[9] Burroughs,
however, always maintained a dry, composed surface in his

early writing, and Kerouac's language in *On the Road* is generally ecstatic and impetuous—more what one would expect from Cassady. Burroughs's influence can be felt, nonetheless, in the book's factuality, its dependence on precise descriptions of life on the road rather than the sentimental impressions in *The Town and the City.*

Burroughs's political and social ideas shape the book's vision of America. Burroughs appears as Old Bull Lee, who has done things "merely for the experience" and now passes his learning to others.[10] His enemies include the federal bureaucracy, liberals, and the police. Old Bull Lee sees America as a police state, and the book shares that vision wholly, portraying police "[peering] out of musty windows" and capable of "[making] the crimes if the crimes don't exist to [their] satisfaction" (*OR,* 136). Conformity and fear have replaced self-reliance and self-esteem. Kerouac's "realization of the fact that something really hard and terrible was coming to America," Ginsberg said, "was the realization that the open road was no longer open for the wandering hobo saint. . . . Kerouac had a very clear and direct picture of that hard military police-state that was descending on America."[11]

No one, not even Lee, has a solution to the repression of the America he describes. *On the Road* involves a search for the father or at least someone who will have the vision and the wisdom that traditionally were the father's, a prophet who will speak "the Word" (*OR,* 55). That prophet seems to be Dean Moriarty, Sr., who, unlike George Martin, chose freedom over work. He has been a hobo, a wanderer, taking a job only when necessary. To Sal Paradise, the book's narrator, Moriarty incarnates the myth of the West. He is also "the father we never found" (*OR*, 310). His spirit dominates the novel, for he represents a rejection of all that is merely respectable, all the domestic and social restraints and values that would make Sal and Dean into good husbands and wage earners. What he rejects is exactly what George Martin and Leo Kerouac respected. In this Western hero, Kerouac envisions a father who could show him what his own father could not.

On the Road is divided into five sections, and all but the last involve Sal's trips west. At first the West seems to offer what he needs. On his first trip, when he is midway between New York and Denver, he wakes up in a skidrow hotel and for a few seconds doesn't know who he is. He has left his eastern past and entered "the West of my future" (*OR*, 17), and it is as if he had become a new person. But then his travels take him to Cheyenne, where Wild West Week is being celebrated, and he knows how far Western traditions and myths have fallen. Later he meets "a shriveled little old man," the "Ghost of the Susquehanna," who shows him that the wilderness is as much a part of the East as of the West (*OR*, 103). By extension, the freedom Sal associates with the West could as well be found near the Susquehanna as the Columbia or the Rio Grande. Moriarty's values can thrive anywhere, and that is what his son shows Sal. The West may have been turned over to the chamber of commerce, but its values, incarnate in Dean, Jr., thrive as much in New York as in San Francisco and Denver.

Dean, says Sal, had been "a young jailkid shrouded in mystery," whose " 'criminality' . . . was a wild yea-saying overburst of American joy" (*OR*, 4, 10). Free of any desire for respectability, he seems a "western kinsman of the sun" with "the tremendous energy of a new kind of American saint" (*OR*, 10, 39). He is "BEAT—the root, the soul of Beatific" (*OR*, 195).

Dean advocates "a whole life of non-interference with the wishes of others, including politicians and the rich." He knows the price for that may be to end, like his father, as a bum, but "there's no harm ending that way" (*OR*, 251). If one doesn't do what is expected, one can't expect the "rewards" that come to those who do. Sal, with his middle-class background, hopes that he and Dean will eventually live near each other with their families. It is a suburban dream that Dean knows to be a compromise, but Sal is in some ways always a tourist in Dean's world; he goes where Dean takes him but always returns to the comfort of his aunt's home back east.

For Dean sex is "the one and only holy and important thing in life" (*OR*, 4), but aside from an idyllic affair with a Mexican field hand named Terry, Sal has very little interest in sex. For him the "holy and important" things are the road itself and bop, the music of "the American night." The road, says Sal, is "life" itself; it is "holy," "unfurling and flying and hissing at incredible speeds across the groaning continent with that mad Ahab at the wheel" (*OR*, 211, 138, 234). This Ahab, "serious and insane at his raving wheel," is in fact the hipster finally free of every law and constraint (*OR*, 299).

Night frees America from responsibility and respectability, and bop, which "was going like mad all over America," has become the "sound of the night" (*OR*, 14). Dean believes that what a great bop musician does is fill "empty space with the substance of our lives." Suddenly "in the middle of a chorus he *gets it.*" Something happens in the music, and everyone understands: "time stops," and it is no longer "the tune that counts but IT" (*OR*, 201). The musician finds something everyone shares; solitude is replaced by a kind of community that doesn't depend on respectability, money, or law.

The road and bop are Sal's primary ways of escaping bureaucratized America, but his greatest moment of transcendence occurs when, seeing a woman sitting in a San Francisco restaurant, he senses that she was his mother in a former life, and stops, "frozen with ecstasy on the sidewalk"(*OR*, 172). He thinks of returning to speak with her, then recalls a vision of his dead father he had experienced a few days earlier, and suddenly finds transcendence, a "complete step across chronological time into timeless shadows" (*OR*, 173). This is the kind of ecstatic moment he wants, and in his search for the release these moments provide, his Mecca promises finally to be Mexico City, "the great and final wild uninhibited Fellahin-childlike city that we knew we would find at the end of the road" (*OR*, 246). Sal does reach Mexico City, but at that point, he become sick, and Dean deserts him to find further adventures back in the north. Sal finds a means to transcendence, only to lose it, and that will be a pattern repeated frequently throughout the rest of Kerouac's fiction. *On the Road* is exactly what a generation of readers took it to be: a guide to ways out of a conformist civilization—but in the end it admits that all these roads lead back to where they began.

Understanding the Beats

There is no final way out. But *On the Road* still has a certain energy and confidence that many of Kerouac's later, darker books do not.

Although *On the Road* was written quickly, with little pause for reflection or revision, it had two and a half years of preparation, plus the example of Cassady's and Burroughs's prose, behind it. A few months after the manuscript was completed, an artist named Ed White suggested that Kerouac write as if he were sketching—responding, that is, immediately and directly to his subject and putting down the words as quickly as they came to his mind. Kerouac did that, and the result was what he called "spontaneous prose." There were obvious similarities here to the improvisation and spontaneity of bop and abstract expressionist painting. In all three instances, the artist attempts an immediate expression without the interference of tradition or sense of what the work should do. The result for Kerouac was what Ginsberg called "Spontaneous Bop Prosody."[12]

Kerouac attempted to explain what he was doing in a "List of Essentials" entitled "Belief & Technique for Modern Prose,"[13] and then clarified his points further in 1953 in "Essentials of Spontaneous Prose." In this essay, first published in 1957, Kerouac said that he would begin with an "image-object" and then allow the language to come in an "undisturbed flow from the mind of personal secret idea-words, *blowing* (as per jazz musicians) on subject of image." He would "[swim] in sea of English with no discipline other than rhythms of exhalation and expostulated statement." Writing " 'without consciousness' in semi-trance" would allow "subconscious to admit in own

uninhibited interesting necessary and so 'modern' language
what conscious art would censor.'' The point was to im-
merse oneself in sound and image and let the words follow
until final revelation or exhaustion brought an end. ''Spontaneous, or ad lib, artistic writing,'' he said elsewhere,
''imitates as best it can the flow of the mind as it moves in
its space-time continuum.''[14]

There are passages throughout Kerouac's work which
revert to the speed writing of *On the Road*. Much of *The
Dharma Bums* is a comparatively orthodox narrative, and
his last novel, *Vanity of Duluoz,* is written in a colloquial
but otherwise conventional style. But spontaneous prose offered Kerouac the richest possibilities, and at its best, as in
The Subterraneans, Tristessa, and ''October in the Railroad
Earth,'' it made possible a complex, evocative prose un-
equaled in kind by any of his contemporaries.

An extreme instance of spontaneous prose is ''Old Angel Midnight'' (written in 1956, published in 1959), in
which words are used primarily for sound rather than
meaning: ''Boy, says Old Angel, this amazing nonsensical
rave of yours wherein I spose you'd think you'd in some
lighter time find hand be-almin ya for the likes of what ya
davote yaself to, pah—bum with a tail only means one
thing,—They know that in sauerkraut bars, god the chew
chew & the wall lips. . . . ''[15]

Kerouac obviously could not have gone much further
without dissolving all syntax and vocabulary into pure abstract sound, a direction followed later in fact by one of his
principal disciples, the poet Clark Coolidge. Clyfford Still,
Jackson Pollock, and other painters followed expressionism
into pure abstraction as did bop musicians, but although

Kerouac was experimenting with essentially the same aesthetic, he never pushed it that far.

Another example of Kerouac's expressionism is his *Book of Dreams* (written from 1952 to 1960, published in 1961), which tries to reveal the essence of dreams in an unmediated flow of language. "Freudianism," Kerouac wrote, "is a big stupid mistaken dealing with causes & conditions instead of the mysterious, essential, permanent reality of Mind Essence." "The fact that everybody in the world dreams every night," he said, "ties all mankind together . . . in one unspoken Union and also proves that the world is really transcendental." Dreams are "naked revelations" of the subconscious, which doesn't discriminate between "good and bad . . . [but] just deals with the realities." As revelations, they are, of course, self-justifying, and what the writer must, therefore, do is simply express them as directly as possible: "so I wrote these dreems [sic] with eerie sleeping cap head."[16]

One of Kerouac's less successful experiments with expressionism was his attempt to create a narrator like those Twain, Anderson, and Faulkner had. The narrator in *Pic* (written in 1951, revised in 1969, published in 1971) is a young black boy, Pictorial Review Jackson, from North Carolina, but although Kerouac had lived briefly in North Carolina with his sister and her family, he knew the Southern dialect primarily from books, and when he tried to duplicate it in *Pic*, the result was caricature: "we sit on the white posts with the shiny buttons in em," Pic says, "and wait 'bout half an hour for the bus, or two half hours, I don't recollect."[17]

Kerouac

Visions of Cody (written in 1951 and 1952, published in 1972) is a much more successful experiment with the possibilities of expressionist aesthetics. There are actually several different narrative and linguistic experiments in the book, each of which embodies a vision or visions of America and Cody Pomeray, the character based on Neal Cassady. None of these experiments is as unsatisfactory as *Pic*, although section three, in which Kerouac merely transcribes a taped discussion with Cassady, is less successful than the rest. The first section of the book consists of sketches involving railroads, diners, B-movies, neon-lit cities, and other aspects of America that can be associated with Cody. It is not an affluent or respectable America but one in which there is greater freedom because there are fewer expectations and fewer rules.

Cody, as described in the second section, seems at first the hero of an adventure book for boys: "where he came from nobody knew or at first cared," yet he is "rough and free" (*VC*, 47, 49). He is the leather-jacketed, muscular, self-reliant young man, who is also "pure-souled" (*VC*, 57).

The narrator, Jack Duluoz, has seen the underside of American life in the neon cities of the East, and in those cities, as his sketches in the first section repeatedly suggest, there is a profound loneliness.[18] That loneliness is reflected in Duluoz himself, who has learned to "accept lostness forever" (*VC*, 33). Cody, however, will not accept lostness, and Duluoz is obsessed with him, seeing in Cody everything that he, Duluoz, can't be: "I'm completely your friend, your 'lover,' " he says, "he who loves you and digs your greatness completely—haunted in the mind by you'' (*VC*, 39).

No man could be all that Duluoz expects of his hero, however, and it is clear from the often dull, rambling conversations in the third section that the "real" Cody is very different from the colossal hero envisioned in the second. That hero could exist only in language, and language becomes the means through which Duluoz can transcend his cloistered solitude. *On the Road* finds transcendence in ceaseless, relentless energy. In *Visions of Cody,* transcendence occurs through words themselves.

The transcription of the tape is followed by "Imitation of the Tape," in which the flatness of the real conversation is replaced by prose similar to that in the first two sections. Eventually it dissolves into a collage of words and sounds like "Old Angel Midnight": "You think I was afraid of them there mawrdegroos in the muckeroo? (Whisper in the audience: Now he's being gay. Answer: Oh, I see, I was wondering what it was all about but from the other side of your thought, my dear)" (*VC*, 273).

"Imitation of the Tape" is followed by "Joan Rawshanks in the Fog," one of Kerouac's most successful attempts at spontaneous prose. Kerouac watched a scene for *Sudden Fear* with Joan Crawford being filmed in San Francisco and used what he saw as the subject for his sketching technique. The result was a defense of language as a more effective medium than movies. "The movies," he says, "have nothing now but great technique to show" (*VC*, 284) and then demonstrates how language can turn the simple process of shooting a scene into complex rhythms and sounds:

Joan Rawshanks, with her long pinched tragic face with its
remaining hints of wild Twenties dissolution, a flapper girl
then, then the writhey girl of the Thirties, under a ramp, in
striped blouse, Anna Lucasta, the girl camping under the
lamp like today you can on a real waterfront see a butch
queer in seamanlongshoreman peacap bowcoat toga, with
simpering fat lips, standing exactly like Joan used to do in
old pictures that followed the Claudette Colbert of *I Covered the Waterfront* (busy little girl). (*VC*, 282)

At the end of the book, Kerouac returns to Cody,
showing him as someone very different from the hero wor-
shiped earlier. He is still an "angel" but he is also Duluoz's
"greatest enemy" (*VC*, 298). Cody, Duluoz realizes, always has to dominate his own world. "Know full well that
I'll never succumb to your advances," Duluoz imagines
Cody telling him (*VC*, 315). But Duluoz's "French-
Canadian side" has its revenge: "Listen," Duluoz tells
himself, "Cody is full of shit; let him go; . . . he's not your
brother, he's not your father, he's not your Saint Michael,
he's a guy, he's married, he works . . . " (*VC*, 362).

The book ends by recounting experiences narrated in
On the Road, but the tone this time is more complex and
less celebratory. Cody is no longer the pure-souled hero he
had seemed. Like all men, he is "blank at last," revealing
no great mystery or insight (*VC*, 397). Cody could not save
Duluoz from "lostness," but in writing about Cody, Du-
luoz/Kerouac had created another, purely linguistic reality.

Kerouac returned to his sketching technique in *Doctor
Sax: Faust Part Three* (written in 1952, published in 1959),
at the beginning of which he says that he had a dream in
which he told himself to "describe the wrinkly tar of this

sidewalk, also the iron pickets of Textile Institute, or the door where Lousy and you and G. J.'s always sittin and dont stop to think of words when you do stop, just stop to think of the picture better—and let your mind off yourself in this work.''[19]

Many of the images and episodes which the novel sketches in this manner are Duluoz's adolescent fantasies with roots in popular movies, radio programs, and magazines. Some of the episodes are hallucinatory: a man with a watermelon suddenly dying a few steps ahead of Duluoz as he walks in the evening with his mother, the stations of the cross mysterious in their dark grotto beside a funeral home, the flooded river that threatens to overrun its banks and destroy the town.

Sometime earlier Duluoz had seen the head on a statue of Sainte Thérèse turn toward him, and once Christ or the Virgin had stood near the boy's bed and pushed it. So he knew he ''was haunted'' long before he first saw his protector Doctor Sax (*DS*, 5). Sax, who wears a shroud for a cape, appears out of the night when Duluoz first becomes aware of sexuality and evil in the world.

Others in Duluoz's fantasies include Count Condu, a vampire from Budapest, living with his retainers in a castle above the town. More fearful is ''the enigma of the New World—the snake of evil whose home is in the deeps of Ecuador and the Amazonian jungle'' (*DS*, 28). This malignant spirit is as old as Indian civilizations, perhaps older. Dr. Sax's job is to protect Duluoz from it.

Cackling gleefully, ''mwee hee hee ha ha,'' Doctor Sax can magically appear anywhere at will. He is Duluoz's ''secret lover,'' ''a mad fool of power, a Faustian man,'' who also has "knowledge of death" (*DS*, 34, 43). Doctor Sax "gets into the blood of children by his cape" (*DS*, 57); he wraps his shroud around them and thereby protects them but at the same time indoctrinates them into the great mysteries from which childhood has protected them.

During the spring when Duluoz is fourteen, the river in his town overflows its banks, and he and his friends want "the Flood to pierce thru and drown . . . the horrible adult routine would" (*DS*, 171). The flood does great damage and shows that nature, not humanity, is master. The boys see "the unaccomplished mud-heap civilization . . . caught with its pants down," an America which has "long lost contact" with its origin in nature (*DS*, 180). Given its chance, nature can overwhelm the city, and nothing can be done except to pile the sandbags higher.

The doctor can show Duluoz the essence of evil, but although Sax speaks "to the bottom of my boy problems and they could all be solved if I could fathom his speech," Duluoz does not at first understand (*DS*, 197). Eventually Sax's meanings become clear, but his wisdom is not enough to defeat the Great World Snake, whose features Duluoz finds outlined in the geography of the town. Sax can, however, show a vision of Judgment Day, when the snake emerges to wreak havoc but is attacked by "the Implacable Bird" and carried "into the Unknown" (*DS*, 243, 245). The lesson to be learned, the doctor says, is simply that "the Universe disposes of its own evil" (*DS*, 245). In the end, there is nothing to fear.

Doctor Sax, expressing both the wild glee and the terrors that come with adolescence, is a boy's book like Mark Twain's *Adventures of Huckleberry Finn* or Robert Louis

Stevenson's *Treasure Island*. Like them, it has the kind of happy ending that is possible only when "real life" is still in the future. In spite of Duluoz's anxieties, *Doctor Sax* is Kerouac's most joyful book. It recreates a secure world of children "playing at latedusk in the yard with aftersupper buzzes and slamming screendoors everywhere" (*DS*, 72). *The Town and the City* deals nostalgically with that world, but in *Doctor Sax* Kerouac's sketching method replaces nostalgia with immediacy. The book is intensely imagined, evoking the experience itself in place of the generalized memories of the earlier novel.

Doctor Sax was written in the summer of 1952. That fall Kerouac wrote a long sketch variously known as "The Railroad Earth," "Wine in the Railroad Earth," and "October in the Railroad Earth," the title by which it is best known. It was published with other short pieces in 1960 in *Lonesome Traveler.* Based on his experiences working as a brakeman for the Southern Pacific, this piece is among Kerouac's most highly regarded works. Landscapes and incidents from his life in San Francisco, where he lived in a skidrow hotel, provided the material for free-form sketching: "There was a little alley in San Francisco back of the Southern Pacific station at Third and Townsend in redbrick of drowsy lazy afternoons with everybody at work in offices in the air you feel the impending rush of their commuter frenzy as soon they'll be charging en masse from Market and Sansome buildings on foot and in buses and all well-dressed thru workingman Frisco. . . ."[20]

Ignoring conventional punctuation in an attempt to maintain the rhythm rather than syntax, "October in the

Railroad Earth'' is a lyrical work that ranges from delicate sweetness to melancholy to ecstatic, visionary joy. An example of the last is the description of the bridge connecting Oakland and San Francisco: ''I'd take walks up Harrison and the boomcrash of truck traffic towards the glorious girders of the Oakland Bay Bridge that you could see after climbing Harrison Hill a little like radar machine of eternity in the sky, huge, in the blue, by pure clouds crossed, gulls, idiot cars streaking to destinations on its undinal boom across shmooshwaters flocked up by winds and news of San Rafael storms and flash boats.''[21]

It is interesting to compare this passage with Hart Crane's vision of Brooklyn Bridge in his poem ''The Bridge,'' where the cables are ''taut miles of shuttling moonlight,'' ''transparent meshes.'' Both Kerouac and Crane achieve great intensity in their language, but Crane's is achieved through dense, rhythmically complex patterns of suggestive sound within a tight stanza. The effect is the result of condensation and revision. Kerouac's intensity, in contrast, is found in the moment and act of writing itself and is expressed in a crescendo of notations. The writing is simultaneous with the vision.

In *Maggie Cassidy* (written in 1953, published in 1959) Kerouac deals again with adolescent memories, but this is not one of his stronger books, in part because Maggie is not a sufficiently interesting character to dominate the work. The book is in fact less about her than about Duluoz's coming of age. At first she seems more sophisticated than he. She thinks they should sleep together, although with the expectation that eventually they will be married.

Duluoz is a high school athlete and is courted by coaches at universities, and with his mother's encouragement, he accepts an offer from Columbia, including a year's training at a prep school in New York. The following spring, Maggie attends his senior prom at the prep school and is miserable, telling him finally, "Oh I hate it here—Jacky let's go back home and sit on the porch . . . I look awful—everything's awful—I knew I shouldnt of come."[22] But New York has greater fascinations for him now: "midnight talks over Brooklyn Bridge, freighters arriving from Montevideo— Wild generations jumping in a jazz joint, hornrimmed geniuses getting drunk on brews" (*MC*, 183). Maggie returns home and does not see him again for three years, and by that time their roles have reversed, and he is too sophisticated for her. He tries to make her sleep with him, but "the sweetness of the girl [is] hidden . . . by a thick rubber girdle at which he [pulls] and [yanks], desperately drunk, poised at the gate." She laughs at him, and after taking her home, he drives away, "skittering crazily in the slush, sick, cursing" (*MC*, 189).

The book's violent and melodramatic ending underscores what it cost Kerouac to become a writer. He could have become a shopkeeper or businessman in Lowell and settled down with someone like Maggie, but that became impossible after he had been swept into "whirlpools of new litter and glitter" (*MC*, 182). *Maggie Cassidy* is a homage to the innocent world Kerouac had abandoned. Family dinners, high school friendships, and small-town gossip are sentimentally and uncritically evoked. The novel is Kerouac's *Tom Sawyer* or *Human Comedy*. It is an idealization of the author's adolescence, a book which, aside from its

Kerouac

conclusion, is very different in mood from the darker considerations of *Doctor Sax*.

In order for Kerouac's sketching method to succeed, it was necessary to have a powerfully suggestive model or subject. In his next novel, he found what he needed in a group of bohemians he knew in New York and in particular a woman he named Mardou Fox.

The Subterraneans is one of Kerouac's major books. Completed, astonishingly, in three days, it follows his memories of an affair with a part-black, part-Indian woman, and his relationships with various writers, artists, and intellectuals, called "the subterraneans" by one of the narrator's friends, Adam Moorad (Ginsberg). People of this sort, says Moorad, "are very quiet, they are very Christ-like."[23] Balliol MacJones (Holmes) calls them "urban Thoreaus" (*S*, 15), but Leo Percepied, the narrator (based on Kerouac himself), is much less sanguine. To him, they have "tendencies to silence, bohemian mystery, drugs, beard, semiholiness," but they are also capable of "insurpassable nastiness" (*S*, 23). The subterraneans use their pacifist attitudes as a kind of protection, attacking others and then retreating into a "non-violent Indian Mahatma Gandhi defense of some kind" that protects them from reprisals (*S*, 77). If anyone tried to attack them physically, they would call the police and "haunt all your dreams" (*S*, 77).

Percepied is fiery and intense—a "big gleeful hood"—while they are cool and withdrawn (*S*, 13). But they always seem sure of themselves, and he lacks self-consciousness. He is the interloper, the outsider who steals their "chick," Mardou, but to him they are "anemic *maquereaux*'' who have never been able to please her (*S*, 23). He is, however, not certain of his own sexual orientation. He has been reading Wilhelm Reich (''the sudden illuminated glad wonderous discovery'' [*S*, 46]), who argued that sexual orgasm is essential as a way of avoiding neurosis. His affair with Mardou is passionate, but he is repeatedly drawn away from her by his mother, by men, and by what he calls ''the asexuality'' of his work as a writer (*S*, 42).

On one occasion, Percepied spends a night ''studying'' a friend's homosexual pornography, later sleeps with a homosexual writer, and is so enchanted with a ''beautiful faun boy'' that Mardou tells Percepied to choose between ''him or me goddamit'' (*S*, 55). Percepied chooses her, but more than either Mardou or the boy, his mother dominates his affections, and toward the end of the book, as he wanders in a freight yard hysterical on the verge of a breakdown, he has a vision of his mother offering ''to take care of you all your days my angel'' (*S*, 104).

Percepied returns to his mother in part because Mardou spends a night with another writer, Yuri Gligoric (Corso). Mardou is one of few women in Kerouac's work who are not incidental to the narrative or who are not, like Maggie Cassidy, treated sentimentally. She is entirely self-reliant, choosing her men as often as she is chosen by them, but when she finally insists on her independence and her right to sleep with Gligoric, Percepied assumes that she no longer loves him. He can see her as many times as he chooses, she says, ''but I want to be independent like I say'' (*S*, 109).

Kerouac

The Subterraneans concludes,

And I go home having lost her love.
And write this book. (*S*, 109)

Mardou has told Percepied that he can stay with her, although on her terms, but what matters finally is his work—not people but the characters he can make of them. In the beginning of the book, Percepied sees himself as Baudelaire (whose mistress, like Mardou, was black), but Mardou tells him, "I would have preferred the happy man to the unhappy poems he's left us" (*S*, 10). At this point Percepied agrees, but as the book progresses, he becomes increasingly obsessed with his work, and Mardou's affair simply gives him the necessary excuse to return to his writing. He says he has received "the essence of her love," and now erects "big word constructions" and in this way betrays that love (*S*, 17).

Like Cody Pomeray, Mardou Fox is transformed into myth. She tells Percepied stories about herself which he makes "the background for thoughts about the Negroes and Indians and America in general but with all the overtones of 'new generation' and other historical concerns" (*S*, 20). In her eyes, he finds "the eventual Kingdom of Inca Maya and vast Azteca shining of gold snake and temples as noble as Greek, Egypt" (*S*, 25). Her life with Percepied becomes a series of imaginative, opulent possibilities for his fiction.

Kerouac chose Percepied as his own name in the novel because the book does not present an objectively detailed sequence of events but rather a record of his often very subjective perceptions. What matters is what he sees and the language which is part of that perception. Bop, he says, is "a mystical unity expressing itself in waves like sinister and again electricity but screaming with palpable aliveness the direct *word* from the vibration, the interchanges of statement, the levels of waving intimation, the smile in sound" (*S*, 34–35). It is just such "levels of waving intimation" and "interchanges of statement," held together in "a mystical unity," that he wants to achieve in its prose, jumping in a seemingly erratic fashion from episode to episode and feeling to feeling but binding them together in the singularity of one central "perception" or vision.

The urgency behind that vision has less to do with specific events in the novel than with the breakdown which threatens him. There is no clear reason or cause for that crisis, although it is clear that his ambivalent sexuality and other personal confusions could devastate him if he did not have his writing to convert everything into a unified understanding or perception. It would not in any case be adequate to approach the cirsis from the perspective of a psychoanalytic model. Salvation is possible only when chaos is transformed into a central, powerful vision.

That expressionistic transformation, effected by writing itself, is never self-conscious. The words must, of course, be immediate, unpremeditated expression, spontaneous and improvised. That does not mean that their ordering is random but that the order derives instantly from intuitive recognition rather than from reflection. Words are consciousness itself rather than an effort to articulate what consciousness has revealed, and the text consequently merges present and past into a single fluid line.

The book is one of Kerouac's most successful attempts at spontaneous writing.[24]

That success owes much to his vision of the woman he calls Mardou. She serves Kerouac in much the way a model would serve an artist, suggesting the painting but not the way it should be executed. The same is true in *Tristessa* (written in 1955 and 1956, published in 1960), in which Kerouac chose for his subject a woman he knew in Mexico. The opening paragraph, spoken by Duluoz, is an especially complex instance of the sketching technique. The paragraph begins and ends with references to Tristessa and in between brings together a wide range of observations and feelings dealing with Mexico City, Duluoz's father, and other matters into a single emotional thread. The structural device is parataxis, juxtaposing a series of observations that simply by virtue of their convergence become a single dense emotional experience, merging melancholy ("the sad vast mist tracks of life") and exhilaration ("Tristessa is high, beautiful as ever"). But Kerouac is also attentive to antithesis in sound and rhythm, and the sentence is a complicated musical structure moving from clauses built from long vowels and slow rhythms (e.g., "lumbering in the sad vast mist tracks of life") to clauses that are very different in sound, as well as feeling ("but now I'm up on that Vegetable plateau Mexico").[25]

The book repeatedly uses such antitheses and extremes to create an emotionally complex narrative. There is, on the one hand, Tristessa herself, whose name means "sadness" and who seems lost in some terrible irremediable anguish, and, on the other, Duluoz, who is driven by passionate desire for her. The first half of the book was written in 1955, the second part a year later. When Kerouac wrote the first, he was studying Buddhism, and Tristessa became his symbol of that suffering from which he believed the Buddha offered redemption, but in the second half she is more a symbol of a fixed desolation at the center of life.

In the first half, Duluoz feels that it may be possible to escape suffering in the world, but in the second half, that hope dissolves in desperation and his recognition that "death is best" (*T*, 81). Drunk, not certain where he is, he follows Tristessa and another woman around Mexico City at night and early in the morning—"everybody curious to see the two ragged girls and the raggedy man, stumbling like a slow team in the dawn" (*T*, 77). It is a view from beyond despair, a view of "grit in the sky" (*T*, 84). Throughout everything, Duluoz keeps returning to his desire to sleep with Tristessa, although it is clear that all she wants are drugs. She is, he says, like "an angel in hell" (*T*, 66). His obsession with her is ultimately pointless; given the choice between morphine and sex, the addict like Tristessa almost without exception chooses the drug.

In his interview with Ted Berrigan, Kerouac pointed to the book's "ingrown-toenail-packed mystical style."[26] The first half of the novel does manifest an intense belief in salvation: "I wish I could communicate to all their combined fears of death," says Duluoz, "the Teaching that I have heard from Ages of Old, that recompenses all that pain with soft reward of perfect silent love abiding . . . in the Void unknown where nothing happens and all simply is what it is" (*T*, 33). "The Buddhas and the Virgin Marys" have given him "proof" that "everything's alright" (*T*, 16). The second half of the book is not so confident. God is present and compassionate ("blessing us with his face which I can only describe as being infinitely sorry"), but compassion alone does not heal or stop the suffering (*T*, 74).

Kerouac had been interested in Buddhism since the early 1950s; early in 1954, he discovered Dwight Goddard's anthology of Buddhist and Taoist texts, *A Buddhist Bible*, and it had a powerful effect on him. As he wrote in *The Dharma Bums*, he was attracted to "the first of Sakyamuni's four noble truths, *All life is suffering*."[27] Buddhism here merely reasserted for Kerouac his traditional Catholic belief that suffering is inevitable, but, he said, he was also "to an extent interested in the third [noble truth], *The suppression of suffering can be achieved*, which I didn't quite believe was possible then" (*DB*, 12). That was in the fall of 1955, and during the following months he read the *Lankavatara Sutra*, studying the doctrine that there is no absolute and that all things are manifestations of the mind. A summer alone as a firespotter in the High Cascades revealed the inner truth of Buddhism and left him, in the words of Jack Duluoz, wanting "to shut up, live, travel, adventure, bless and dont be sorry."[28] But he also found that, at least for himself it was not possible to extinguish suffering. Buddhism failed him in that, as it also failed to provide him with the sense of "a Personal God" that Catholicism gave. Even when his interest in Buddhism was strongest, he found himself "wishing there were a Personal God in all this impersonal matter" (*DB*, 186). He returned eventually to the Catholic Church, but as late as 1967, in his interview with Berrigan, he claimed that Buddhism had influenced him "almost as much as Catholicism."[29]

Between 1954 and 1956, Kerouac devoted much of his writing to poetry and to works about Buddhism, but very little of this has been published, and so it is difficult to gauge the depth of his understanding of Buddhism and the degree to which its view of life as suffering merely reinforced similar beliefs in his Catholic background. Philip Whalen, who knew Kerouac well at this time, said that Kerouac's "interest in Buddhism was pretty much literary."[30] It may be impossible to determine how well Kerouac understood Buddhism until his letters and manuscripts, currently restricted by his estate, are released. His interest in Buddhism was unquestionably sincere, but his Catholic sense of suffering and death as the penalty for sin not only did not recede but also reasserted itself with increased certainty in *Tristessa, Desolation Angels*, and *Big Sur.*

One of Kerouac's major Buddhist projects, running apparently to a thousand pages, still unpublished, is a work entitled "Some of the Dharma," in which he included his own translations of sutras from translations that had been made into French. He wrote a life of the Buddha, also still unpublished, which is variously called "Wake Up" and "Buddha Tells Us." His one major Buddhist work which has been published is *The Scripture of the Golden Eternity,* a "sutra" written for Gary Snyder which suggests that Kerouac at least understood the fundamental paradox of Buddhism, that all experience is essentially emptiness; that purity and absence are one. The sutra does not deny God, however, but identifies Him with the self. It also declares that heaven is to be found in the present moment, a belief to which Kerouac returned in *Visions of Gerard*. The sutra asserts that the world is without moral identity, and, therefore, "do what you want." "The world," Kerouac says, "is nothing but a dream and is just thought of and the everlasting eternity pays no attention to it."[31]

Most of Kerouac's poetry is also unpublished, though his major poetic work, *Mexico City Blues*, appeared in 1959 and has never been out of print. Allen Ginsberg called it "a great classic" constructed "with a self-invented poetics" (*Composed*, 64). Michael McClure argued that the book is Kerouac's "masterpiece . . . , a religious poem startling in its majesty and comedy and gentleness and vision." McClure felt that there was "no doubt" that *Mexico City Blues* was to be Kerouac's "own equivalent" to Pound's *Cantos*. But while Pound wanted to restore past traditions, to make them new, Kerouac's epic is a poem outside history, a record of discrete illuminations in the present. He was creating, as McClure said, "a mystical (in its hope), anarchist, epic-length, and open-ended poem."[32]

In a note at the beginning of the book, Kerouac says that he wants "to be considered a jazz poet blowing a long blues in an afternoon jazz session on Sunday,"[33] and the individual poems depend, like jazz pieces, on spontaneity and inspiration. Each of the 242 "choruses" is limited by the size of the notebook pages on which he wrote; if an idea (or riff) was not exhausted in that space, he would pick it up in the next poem. On the other hand, the 11th chorus stops at the end of five lines, and at the bottom of the page after a long break, Kerouac says, in parentheses, that the musician wasn't playing; he was "brooding" (*MCB*, 11).

Most of the choruses are playful and light, and seemingly anything that fits the general drift of the rhythm, music, and tone can be added, no matter how incongruous it may seem: the sound of a bus outside the building ("Z a r o o o m o o o"), an idea for Buddhist lipstick ("Nirvana-No"), nonsense language ("I'm an Agloon") (*MCB*, 73, 201, 50). The poems' achievement lies in the ability to incorporate disparate resources into delicate music without ever becoming simply a cacophony of sounds. "Lies are heavier than your intentions," Kerouac said. "And your confessions lighter than Heaven." The poem, for him, was a confession, a deeply personal statement.[34] The admission might be specific (as in the 149th chorus where Kerouac expresses his love for his mother), but usually in *Mexico City Blues* it is a more general revelation about feelings or impressions. In any case, the poem expresses the poet's sensibility at the moment of writing, and the final poem identifies "the sound in your mind" as an origin for song (*MCB*, 244).

McClure points to "the beautifully controlled energy" of *Mexico City Blues*, but the source of that control is not perhaps immediately evident. The poems obviously do not depend on conventions of form and meter. In Ginsberg's words, "Mind is shapely, Art is shapely. Meaning Mind practiced in spontaneity invents forms in its own image." Or, as seen from another perspective by Gregory Corso, "The poet and the poetry are inseparable."[35]

Kerouac also worked on many other blues sequences, "San Francisco Blues," "Orlando Blues," "MacDougal Street Blues," and others that he wanted to collect eventually in a single volume. It is unfortunate for the understanding of Kerouac that so few of his Buddhist writings have been made public, but the fact that so little of the poetry has been published is much more serious. Kerouac is so widely known as a novelist that his poetry is generally overlooked. Various blues from the MacDougal Street, Orizaba, Orlando, and San Francisco sequences can be found in *Scattered Poems* (1971) and *Heaven & Other Poems,* however. Perhaps when all the Kerouac manuscripts are finally released for publication, it will be as impossible to avoid Kerouac in any discussion of the poetry of the period as it is to avoid Olson or Ginsberg or Creeley.

Kerouac considered his novels as contributions to "one vast book like Proust's."[36] The subject was "the Duluoz legend," a fictionalization of events from his own life. Chronologically arranged in this fashion, *Visions of Gerard* (written in 1956, published in 1963) would be read first. In Proust's *Remembrance of Things Past,* however, one insight or memory seems to unfold directly out of another, and it is, therefore, necessary to read the books chronologically, but that is not the case with "the Duluoz legend." It is more important to read Kerouac's novels in the order of their composition as they reflect important changes in Kerouac's aesthetic and thinking.[37] Although *Visions of Gerard* is the first volume in "the Duluoz legend," it was written during Kerouac's Buddhist period and involves a more mature understanding than the earlier works.

Visions of Gerard, Kerouac's gentlest book, is a homage to his brother, who died from a rheumatic heart at the age of nine. A few months before his death, Gerard had a vision of the Virgin Mary coming to take him to heaven, and nuns, thinking he had been blessed, gathered at his deathbed to hear his final words.

Gerard believed the meaning of his vision to be simply, "we're all in Heaven——but we dont know it!" (*VG*, 68) Heaven existed for him in perfect love for all living things. He was Christ-like. At the time Kerouac wrote the novel, he believed "the good news [to be] that Nirvana, Heaven, Our Salvation is *Here* and *Now*" (*VG*, 130). Buddhism was a "re discovery" of truths he had learned in childhood from his brother: "All is Well, practice Kindness, Heaven is Nigh" (*VG*, 13–14).

In spite of this, the book retains Kerouac's Catholic sense of humanity stained by sin. The world is imbued with evil: "sin is sin and there's no erasing it——We are spiders. We sting one another" (*VG*, 42). Only Gerard with his vision of transcendence, his discovery of a heaven out of suffering, offers consolation.

The book ends with Gerard's burial. The narrator remembers himself as he was then, four years old, sitting in a car a few feet from the grave as the coffin was lowered into the earth. His mother and sister "burst out sobbing," and he turned to them to ask "Well why are you crying?" (*VG*, 151). The weight of the novel rests on that question. He was told that he was "too young to understand," but he understood better than they the finality of death. His brother had taught him that what matters is the present moment. He looked out the car window and saw an "old gravedigger [pick] up his shovel and [close] the book" (*VG*, 151). "Death," as the narrator had said earlier, "is the only decent subject, since it marks the end of illusion and delusion" (*VG*, 123).

Kerouac

Kerouac's father (Emil Alcide Duluoz) is characterized affectionately in this novel, but like George Martin in
The Town and the City, Emil is an innocent victim, no more
able to prevent his son's suffering than Martin could prevent economic failure. Unable to control his world, Emil
responds by drinking, playing cards, joking with friends,
and in general finding what pleasure he can. Gerard is
equally a victim, but if he cannot control life, he can transform it with love.

Kerouac's works follow an emotional curve which
crests in works written between the spring of 1954, when
he discovered Goddard's book, and the summer of 1956,
when he worked as a fire lookout in the High Cascades.
With the exception of *The Dharma Bums,* the books written
after his return from the mountain—particularly the second
half of *Tristessa, Desolation Angels,* and *Big Sur*—are
somber, desperate works.

Duluoz, at the beginning of *Desolation Angels* (written in 1956 and 1961, published in 1965), has "come face
to face" with himself and sees his life as "a vast inconse-
quential epic" (*DA,* 4, 12). He has spent a summer in solitude in the High Cascades on Desolation Peak and wants
now only to leave, get a haircut and a new black leather
jacket, and "regain [his] love of life" (*DA,* 5). In fact,
when Kerouac returned from the mountain, the Beats were
about to become news. "Howl" would not be published
until that fall, and *On the Road* not for another year, but
Ginsberg and his friends were already well enough known
to be photographed for *Mademoiselle,* and the *New York
Times* had carried a laudatory article by Richard Eberhart,

describing "Howl" as "a powerful work," which "lays bare the nerves of suffering and spiritual struggle."[38] Kerouac would soon be a celebrity, and *Desolation Angels* is the record of his discovery that he could not live the quiet life he had imagined for himself before leaving the mountain.

The Buddhist influence at the beginning of the book is still deep, pervading Duluoz with an awareness of void and silence, but now he identifies the void with desolation. Buddhism has not released him from suffering but made him more aware of his own anguish: "I see it, I suffer, we all suffer, people die in your arms" (*DA*, 170–71).

Desolation Angels is really two novels, the first of which, originally entitled "The Angels in the World," was written immediately following the events it describes. The second "Beat Traveler," was written five years later. In the intervening years, the Beats had become celebrities, and "Beat Traveler" is a meditation on the costs. When Kerouac returned from Desolation Peak, he wanted to find peace "as a man of contemplations rather than too many actions," "to see the world from the viewpoint of solitude and to meditate upon the world without being imbroglio'd in its actions, which have by now become famous for their horror & abomination" (*DA*, 219–20), but as the "King of the Beats," as he would be known, his life was repeatedly interrupted by journalists and admirers.

On the Road received an extraordinarily favorable review by Gilbert Millstein in the 5 September 1957 issue of the *New York Times*. Millstein thought the novel bore a relation to the Beat Generation much like that which *The Sun Also Rises* had to the 1920s. A second, rather negative, review appeared in the *Times* a few days later but could not stem the enthusiasm the novel had already aroused. Few critics would be as favorably disposed toward Kerouac as Millstein, but the book's reputation did not depend on their opinion. Kerouac was suddenly a celebrity, and there were rumors that his book would soon be turned into a movie starring Marlon Brando.

Kerouac's fame was important in that it brought his work to the attention of younger writers such as Clark Coolidge, Sam Shepard, and Tom Robbins. At the same time, however, Kerouac's television appearances and references to him in the newspapers, *Time, Life,* and *Newsweek* created a following which was less interested in his books than in his autograph. For Kerouac, the result, recorded in *Desolation Angels,* was a period of deep depression.

Visiting Bull Hubbard (Burroughs) in Tangiers, Duluoz turns "from a youthful brave sense of adventure to a complete nausea concerning experience in the world at large" (*DA,* 300). He feels "that awful revulsion for everything," "the mistakes everywhere the mistakes" (*DA,* 302). To keep traveling, to stay on the road, would at this point mean only going further "into the darkness of the fearful heart" (*DA,* 303). Nonetheless, when he returns to America, he takes his mother by bus to California in what would seem almost a parody, were it not so troubled and pathetic, of Kerouac's earlier life with Cassady. He looks for the world he knew and finds instead a "prosperous America," in which people laugh at him and his mother in their evident poverty.

When they reach San Francisco, he slowly begins to see things as she does. She tells him that "California is sinister," and seeing the Golden Gate Bridge makes him *"shudder with horror.* The bottom drops out of my soul. Something about that bridge, something *sinister* like Ma says" (*DA,* 352, 353). She tells him finally that they should go back to their home in the East, and he decides to "follow [her] because she speaks of *tranquillity*" (*DA,* 360). His mother, he says, "provided me with the means for peace and good sense" (*DA,* 336), and peace is what he needs.

In abandoning California and the open road, Kerouac signifies the end of a central American myth. "A peaceful sorrow at home is the best I'll ever be able to offer the world, in the end," Duluoz says at the close of the novel, "and so I told my Desolation Angels goodbye. A new life for me" (*DA,* 366). That new life is, of course, the antithesis of the hipster's. The adventure which began when Kerouac met Burroughs ended here.

Desolation Angels is a joyless book. The prose is powerful in its long, plaintive meditations on the inevitability of suffering, but there is no relief from it except in "peaceful sorrow." Buddhism promised Kerouac an end to suffering but revealed instead that there was no meaning, no explanation for the way things are: "There's your Actual Void Face—exactly what this empty universe holds in store for us, the Blank—Blank, Blank, Blank" (*DA,* 115). The book is the record of a man crucified by his recognition that he cannot escape suffering, that the best he can expect is the solace offered by the home and the values from which years ago he had fled.

Although Kerouac considered *The Dharma Bums* a potboiler, it is, aside from *On the Road,* the book for which he is best known. It was written a year after the first part of *Desolation Angels* but deals with his experiences immediately before the incidents related in that book.

Looking back on his earlier life, the narrator Ray Smith (based on Kerouac himself) says, "I was very devout in those days and was practicing my religious devotions almost to perfection. Since then I've become a little hypocritical about my lip-service and a little tired and cynical" (*DB*, 6). The principal figure in the novel, however, is Japhy Ryder (Gary Snyder), whose Buddhism is never shaken. Furthermore, he foresees "a world full of rucksack wanderers, Dharma Bums refusing to subscribe to the general demand that they consume production and therefore have to work for the privilege of consuming" (*DB*, 77–78). For a while Smith tries to share Ryder's beliefs and optimism and insists that "everything is possible. I am God, I am Buddha, I am imperfect Ray Smith, all at the same time, I am empty space, I am all things"(*DB*, 97).

Japhy, "the rucksack revolution," and Smith's quest for enlightenment made *The Dharma Bums* seem especially relevant in the 1960s, but there is another side to the book somewhat less optimistic and utopian. Rosie, another of Smith's friends, sees America as a police state. While Japhy foresees "a great rucksack revolution," Rosie believes there will be "a big new revolution of police" (*DB*, 87). In great depression, she kills herself. If, however, she had done more than talk about her fears, Smith believes, she might have remained alive. Those who don't take risks in America end like Rosie in madness. "The only alternative to sleeping out, hopping freights, and doing what I wanted," Smith says, " . . . would be to just sit with a hundred other patients in front of a nice television set in a madhouse, where we would be 'supervised' " (*DB,* 96). Then, however, he realizes "the truth Rosie knew now"— the truth which only the dead know and which is "beyond the Tree of Buddha as well as the Cross of Jesus" (*DB,* 108). He realizes that in death is something "everlastingly tranquil and blissful" (*DB,* 110), that in the end there is no suffering. He understands why she chose suicide. Freedom, he realizes, comes from knowing that there is no answer except the silent grave.

At the end of *The Dharma Bums* Smith asserts that "the vision of the freedom of eternity was mine forever" (*DB,* 190), but that freedom is the one which Rosie, not Japhy, taught him: "nothing *is* nothing" (*DB,* 188). Japhy, for his part, knows that Smith will eventually desert Buddhism for Christianity. "Oh, don't start preaching Christianity to me," Japhy says, "I can just see you on your deathbed kissing the cross" (*DB,* 159).

In fact, Kerouac's next book, *Big Sur,* is profoundly Christian. Written in ten consecutive nights in the fall of 1961 and published the following year, it concerns Kerouac's visit to California a year earlier, shortly after the second half of *Desolation Angels* was finished. Ostensibly he went in order to work on the manuscript of *Book of Dreams* for Lawrence Ferlinghetti (Lorenzo Monsanto in *Big Sur*), who was planning to publish it at City Lights Press. Ferlinghetti offered his cabin in Big Sur's Bixby Canyon (here called Raton Canyon), where Kerouac could be alone, uninterrupted by his worshipful followers. He was now almost forty, twice the age of many who had read *On the Road* and *The Dharma Bums* and thought of him as their spiritual leader, and as Duluoz puts it in *Big Sur,* he was "sick and tired of all the endless enthusiasms of new young kids trying to know me and pour out all their lives into me" (*BS*, 109).

Raton Canyon is spanned by a bridge a thousand feet above the ground. Upended in the sand below is the rusted chassis of a car which plunged off the bridge ten years before, and its wreck is effectively the symbol of Duluoz's life on the road. This time in fact he has come west on the train in a private compartment. He is a successful writer who is able to pay the bill for a group of casual acquaintances at a restaurant or give his friend Cody enough to cover the rent, but he no longer believes in the things which used to sustain him.

After three weeks at the cabin, Duluoz decides to hitchhike north to see friends in San Francisco. The road above the canyon is jammed, however, with cars of tourists, who "see in [him] the very apotheosical opposite of their every vacation dream and of course drive on" (*BS*, 46). None of these fathers and husbands will be exploring the "Big Two Hearted River" or "the silent secret roads of America" (*BS*, 45). They are the successful bureaucrats, managers, and professionals, and as a well-known writer, Kerouac was, in a sense, one of them; but their vision of America had nothing to do with his. The tourists look out their windows at Duluoz and imagine that he might be "the Hollywood hitchhiker with the hidden gun" (*BS*, 47). Only toward the end of the day does anyone stop for him. It was, he says, the last time he ever hitchhiked.

Before going to San Francisco, Duluoz experiences "the form of horror of an eternal condition of sickmortality" (*BS*, 41). It is the beginning of a breakdown which reaches a crisis shortly after he returns to the canyon. The breakdown is, on the one hand, brought on by acute alcoholism, but it involves as well the breakdown of all the beliefs and ideas with which he has sustained himself. Confronted with the reality and inevitability of annihilation, he feels "completely nude of all poor protective devices like thoughts about life or meditations under trees and the 'ultimate' " (*BS*, 41). As the crisis intensifies, he becomes increasingly paranoid, believing that the local creek has been poisoned with kerosene, that his friends are trying to kill him, and even that his girlfriend's four-year-old son is a warlock. He is unnerved by the winds that roar through the canyon, and the cabin feels "haunted" (*BS*, 179).

As a child, Duluoz imagined that people were laughing at him and that he was the only one who did not know "the secret of the world," but Jesus was not "peeking down my neck'——There lies the root of my belief in Jesus" (*BS*, 116). As an adult he began to think of himself "as a special solitary angel sent down as a messenger from Heaven to tell everybody or show everybody by example that their peeking society was actually the Satanic Society and they were all on the wrong track" (*BS*, 117). He began seeing himself in messianic terms, his writings as revelatory and his role as that of a prophet. And "if I dont write what actually I see happening in this unhappy globe which is rounded by the contours of my deathskull I think I'll have been sent on earth by poor God for nothing" (*BS*, 167). Writing is in short like confession, which in the Catholic Church precedes penance, the sacrament through which a person is absolved of sin.

Kerouac

At the furthest depth of his anguish, Duluoz has a vision of the cross: "my body starts dying and swooning out to the Cross standing in a luminous area of the darkness" (*BS*, 205). The book ends with a vision of "simple golden eternity blessing all." However, the final sentence, "There's no need to say another word," would be an ominous pronouncement for any writer, and it was especially so for Kerouac, who had until now transcended his private anguish by transforming it into fiction (*BS*, 216). He had found that "the world is too old for us to talk about it with our new words" (*BS*, 35). Kerouac would write more books, but they would not have the conviction and urgency of the earlier work.

Sartori in Paris (written in 1965, published in 1966) is among Kerouac's weakest books, but it is important as an indication of the kind of man Kerouac had become, or wanted to become, after he deserted his earlier values and returned permanently to his mother's house. *Sartori* is the Buddhist term for enlightenment, but the enlightenment Kerouac is in search of here has nothing to do with Eastern religion. The book, which is the only one Kerouac wrote in which he used his own name for the protagonist, deals with his visit to Brittany in 1965 in search of his family roots and should be read as a reaffirmation of his father's heritage and values. "I'm not a Buddhist," Kerouac says, "I'm a Catholic revisiting the ancestral land that fought for Catholicism against impossible odds yet won in the end."[39]

The surface of the narrative is gentle and bemused. The narrator claims to be descended from the princes of Brittany but knows that he is not their equal, that his home is in the tavern, not the court. He tries to see himself as a comic figure and not the spiritually tortured Jack Duluoz of *Big Sur,* but the pain still surfaces. He is a "boneyard of decay," he says—"scared and humbled" (*SP,* 78).

The climactic episode involves a visit to a distant relative, a restaurateur in Brittany confined to his bed to recover from a hernia operation, the penalty for hard work. The episode has an obvious irony: the King of the Beats, the man responsible for sending a generation "on the road," makes a connection to his ancestral past in the person of a conventional middle-class businessman who has been working too hard.

Raymond Baillet, the cabdriver who takes Kerouac to the airport, is also working hard to support his family. Kerouac says that Baillet may have been "the cause of my sartori in Paris," and although the nature of that sartori or enlightenment is never exactly specified, it is likely that it had to do with the fact that Baillet "was polite, kind, efficient, hip, aloof, and many other things and mainly just a cabdriver who happened to drive me to Orly airfield on my way back home from France" (*SP,* 8). Baillet might be compared to Cody; both are excellent drivers (Baillet goes "90 in the rain slick highway" [*SP,* 118]), but while one is a man of visions and freedom, the other does his job, supports his family, and has no pretensions.

Saroyan's autobiographical works may have influenced the book. *Sartori in Paris* is like the works he was writing at this time: *The Bicycle Rider in Beverly Hills* (1952), *Short Drive Sweet Chariot* (1966), and other books of anecdotal reminiscences generally concerned with traveling, day-to-day experiences, and particularly ethnic identity. Compared with Saroyan's earlier books, these later ones seem mellow, as if the author had resolved most of his problems with the world and was willing now to accept things as they are. *Sartori in Paris* also seems the work of a man who has made his peace with the world, but in fact at this time, Kerouac's health was poor, he was drinking heavily, and, as he wrote soon after completing the book, "now my hand doesn't move as fast as it used to."[40] His major works depend on perfect honesty, and *Sartori in Paris* is not altogether an honest book. In spite of attempts at geniality and humor, there is a desperation in Kerouac's accounts of his heavy drinking, his search for a relative (literally any relative), and his sudden decision to return home. He was in fact a haunted, desperate man.

Kerouac's last novel, in which he returned to the subject matter he had used in his first, is *Vanity of Duluoz: An Adventurous Education, 1935–46* (1968). The book is a monologue addressed to his wife Stella, whom he had married a few months earlier. She was the sister of a high school friend and had known many of the same people that Kerouac did, so he could talk informally, and the tone of the book is gentle and relaxed, very different from that of *The Town and the City.*

The narrator is again Duluoz, who wants to show his wife why he has become the kind of person he is. The initial cause, he says, was the kind of people he had to deal with, but then he adds that people are so different from the way they had been thirty years earlier that he doesn't "recognize them as people any more or recognize myself as a real member of something called the human race."[41]

As in *The Town and the City,* the central conflict involves a father and son. Emil Duluoz, like George Martin, cannot understand why his values are not his son's. In spite of failures, Emil still believes that one should make the best of things. His son, however, is friendly with three young men from New Orleans, Wilson Holmes Hubbard, Franz Mueller, and the young man Mueller loves, Claude de Maubris (based, respectively, on Burroughs, Kammerer, and Carr). Duluoz, like his father, is a New England idealist, but his friends are reserved, skeptical, and realistic. "Their style was dry, new to me," Duluoz says; "mine had been the misty-nebulous New England Idealist style tho (as I say) my saving grace in their eyes (Will's, Claude's especially) was the materialistic Canuck taciturn cold skepticism all the picked-up Idealism in the world of books couldnt hide" (*VD*, 207–8).

In their company, Duluoz becomes the realistic "Canuck" he believes he fundamentally is rather than a "New England Idealist" like his father. In fact, in much of his of earlier work, Kerouac is very much an idealist, searching for ways to transcend suffering. His life on the road, his Buddhism, and his writing were ways of transcending or at least transforming his past, but *Desolation Angels,* the second half of *Tristessa, Big Sur,* and *Sartori in Paris* all involve a rejection of that earlier idealism and the reassertion of the values and attitudes which he associated with a "Canuck" and Catholic heritage. In *Vanity of Duluoz,* his friends lead him back to his father's world as it might have been before it was overlaid with New England optimism and ideals. *Vanity of Duluoz* affirms suffering as the fundamental and unavoidable fact of life. Duluoz says that he and his father thought "the only good thing . . . [that] had ever happened to us was that we could fall asleep at night and dream, and the only bad thing, wake up to this gnashing world'' (*VD*, 257).

Finally, Duluoz begins "to get a new vision of my own of a truer darkness which just overshadowed all this overlaid mental garbage of 'existentialism' and 'hipsterism' and 'bourgeois decadence' '' (*VD*, 273). It is a vision of ''a mean heartless creation emanated by a God of Wrath'' and is confirmed by his father's agonizing illness and death from cancer (*VD*, 274). Death leaves Duluoz alone in private agony: '' 'Father, Father, why hast thou forsaken me?' for real, the man who gave you hopeful birth is copping out right before your eyes and leaves you flat with the whole problem and burden (your self) of his own foolishness in ever believing that 'life' was worth anything but what it smells like down in the Bellevue Morgue'' (*VD*, 274).

For Duluoz, the only adequate release from suffering is compassion and religious faith. As in *Big Sur*, he has a vision of the cross, and the book ends with a reaffirmation of Kerouac's Catholic belief. On the final page Duluoz tells his wife that he wants his ''chalice'' filled with wine. He means, of course, both wine to bury the agonies of his world today and the wine which, in the sacrament of the Eucharist, becomes the blood of Christ.

Shortly before his death, Kerouac decided to write a novel about his father, which would be called ''The Spotlight Print,'' the name of Leo Kerouac's lithography business. If *Vanity of Duluoz* is an indication, the new book would have further rejected values associated with Dean Moriarty and the hipster—temporary solutions, Kerouac now believed, which obscured the fact that in the end there were no panaceas or escape.

Burroughs had in fact told him that when he first considered Buddhism as a solution. In a letter written to Kerouac in August, 1954, Burroughs wrote that "in my usual sloppy way to be sure," he had "studied and practiced Buddhism" but seen it finally as an escape, "shivering in cosmic winds on a bare mountain slope above life-line." Whatever Buddhism offered the East, it was no solution for the West, where one had to "learn by acting, experiencing, and living; that is, above all, by *Love* and by *Suffering*." [42]

Notes

1. Jack Kerouac, *Visions of Gerard* (New York: Farrar, Straus, 1963) 132. Subsequent references are given parenthetically in the text.

2. Jack Kerouac, *Visions of Cody* (New York: McGraw-Hill, 1972) 23. Subsequent references are given parenthetically in the text.

3. Warren G. French has noted that Kerouac told one of his readers in 1950 that he was both Francis and Peter and also something of Joe, although French sees the latter as owing more to Neal Cassady (*Jack Kerouac* [Boston: Twayne, 1986] 25). According to Gerald Nicosia, "Early in the novel's composition, Jack told Allen that he was splitting his mind into discrete parts and embodying each part in a different person" (*Memory Babe: A Critical Biography of Jack Kerouac* [New York: Grove, 1983] 303).

4. Jack Kerouac, *The Town and the City* (New York: Harcourt, Brace, 1950) 67, 68. Subsequent references are given parenthetically in the text.

5. French, *Jack Kerouac*, 28–29.

6. "Kerouac was a regular prose writer writing in the forms of Thomas Wolfe; that is to say, long, symphonic-sentenced, heavy-voweled periods, a little with echo of Milton" (Allen Ginsberg, *Allen Verbatim: Lectures on Poetry, Politics, Consciousness*, ed. Gordon Ball [New York: McGraw-Hill, 1974] 151–52). Warren Tallman hears popular music of the 1930s in the style of *The Town and the City* ("Kerouac's Sound," *On the Road: Text and Criticism*, ed. Scott Donaldson [New York: Viking, 1979] 520).

7. For a history of the book's development, see Timothy A. Hunt, *Kerouac's Crooked Road: Development of a Fiction* (Hamden, CT: Archon, 1981). On Kerouac's response to Viking, see Jack Kerouac and John Clellon Holmes, "To Europe and Return," *Kerouac and the Beats,* ed. Arthur and Kit Knight (New York: Paragon, 1988) 138. Holmes said the book originally was "a third longer" (Tytell, "Holmes," 153). Ginsberg, however, insisted that Kerouac had not really followed the publisher's suggestions, and the original manuscript and published book were "not very different" (James McKenzie, "An Interview with Allen Ginsberg," *Kerouac and the Beats,* 251).

8. Ted Berrigan, "The Art of Fiction XLI: Jack Kerouac," *On the Road: Text and Criticism,* ed. Donaldson, 541; Allen Ginsberg, Review of *The Dharma Bums, Village Voice,* 12 November 1958, 3.

9. Berrigan, "Jack Kerouac," 541; Jack Kerouac, "Letter to Neal Cassady," *Kerouac and the Beats,* ed. Arthur and Kit Knight, 130.

10. Jack Kerouac, *On the Road* (New York: Viking, 1957) 143.

11. McKenzie, "Ginsberg," 238.

12. Ginsberg, Review of *The Dharma Bums,* 4.

13. Jack Kerouac, *Heaven & Other Poems* (San Francisco: Grey Fox, 1977) 46–47.

14. Jack Kerouac, "Essentials of Spontaneous Prose," *On the Road: Text and Criticism,* ed. Donaldson, 531–33; Tom Clark, ed. *Kerouac's Last Word: Jack Kerouac in Escapade* (Sudbury, MA: Water Row, 1986) 47.

15. Jack Kerouac, "Old Angel Midnight," *Big Table* 1 (Spring 1959): 10.

16. Jack Kerouac, *Book of Dreams* (San Francisco: City Lights, 1961) 158, 3, 4.

17. Jack Kerouac, *Pic* (New York: Grove, 1971) 42.

18. This is Kerouac's first book to be narrated by Jack Duluoz, the name he used in most of his work for the character he modeled on himself. "Duluoz," he said, was a variation ("invented just for fun") of "that old Breton name Daoulas" (Jack Kerouac, *Sartori in Paris* [New York: Grove, 1966] 101).

19. Jack Kerouac, *Doctor Sax: Faust Part Three* (New York: Grove, 1959) 3. Subsequent references are given parenthetically in the text.

20. Jack Kerouac, "October in the Railroad Earth," *Lonesome Traveler* (New York: Grove, 1960) 37.

21. Kerouac, "October in the Railroad Earth," 43. Kerouac's preference for rhythm over syntax is especially evident in the segment he recorded with Steve Allen providing a bop accompaniment on piano (*Poetry for the Beat Generation,* Hanover, 1959). The complete Kerouac recordings are available in *The Jack Kerouac Collection* (Rhino Records, 1990).

Understanding the Beats

22. Jack Kerouac, *Maggie Cassidy* (New York: Avon, 1959) 177.

23. Jack Kerouac, *The Subterraneans* (New York: Grove, 1958) 1. Subsequent references are given parenthetically in the text.

24. When MGM decided to film *The Subterraneans*, they asked Saroyan, whom Kerouac greatly admired, to write the screenplay. Saroyan considered the offer but finally turned it down. The movie itself suggests that Hollywood was not ready for a film about a black woman and a white man. Leslie Caron was cast as Mardou Fox; Percepied was played by George Peppard.

25. Jack Kerouac, *Tristessa* (New York: McGraw-Hill, 1960) 3. Subsequent references are given parenthetically in the text.

26. Berrigan, "Jack Kerouac," 543.

27. Jack Kerouac, *The Dharma Bums* (New York: Viking, 1958) 12. Subsequent references are given parenthetically in the text.

28. Jack Kerouac, *Desolation Angels* (New York: Coward-McCann, 1965) 5. Subsequent references are given parenthetically in the text.

29. Berrigan, "Jack Kerouac," 556.

30. Barry Gifford and Lawrence Lee, *Jack's Book: An Oral Biography of Jack Kerouac* (New York: St. Martin's, 1978) 217.

31. Jack Kerouac, *The Scripture of the Golden Eternity* (New York: Totem/Corinth, 1960), verses 42, 62.

32. Michael McClure, *Scratching the Beat Surface* (San Francisco: North Point, 1982) 71, 72, 75.

33. Jack Kerouac, *Mexico City Blues* (New York: Grove, 1959) iii. Subsequent references are given parenthetically in the text.

34. Jack Kerouac, Statement on poetics, *The New American Poetry,* ed. Donald M. Allen (New York: Grove, 1960) 414. This is not, of course, to say that Kerouac was a "confessional poet" like Anne Sexton or W. D. Snodgrass. Kerouac was concerned with immediacy of expression, and his expressionist technique necessarily made the poem a personal statement, but he was not interested in poetry as psychological revelation and indeed, as indicated above, had little or no regard for Freudian thought.

35. McClure, *Scratching the Beat Surface,* 75. Allen Ginsberg, "Notes for *Howl* and Other Poems," *The New American Poetry,* ed. Donald M. Allen, 415. Robert King, "Gregory Corso," *The Beat Vision* ed. Arthur and Kit Knight (New York: Paragon, 1987) 154.

36. Jack Kerouac, *Big Sur* (New York: Farrar, Strauss and Cudahy, 1962) iii. Subsequent references are given parenthetically in the text.

37. Regina Weinreich argued this point, showing that the books are best read as a series of experiments resolving problems in Kerouac's aesthetic. See *The Aesthetics of Spontaneity: A Study of the Fiction of Jack*

Kerouac (Carbondale: Southern Illinois University Press, 1987). My own understanding of Kerouac's development as a writer is strongly indebted to Weinreich's book.

38. Richard Eberhart, "West Coast Rhythms," *New York Times Book Review,* 2 September 1956, 8.

39. Jack Kerouac, *Sartori in Paris* (New York: Grove, 1966) 69. Subsequent references are given parenthetically in the text.

40. Clark, ed., *Kerouac's Last Word,* 48.

41. Jack Kerouac, *Vanity of Duluoz* (New York: Coward-McCann, 1968) 7. Subsequent references are given parenthetically in the text.

42. William S. Burroughs, *Letters to Allen Ginsberg: 1953–1957* (New York: Full Court, 1982) 56–57.

CHAPTER THREE

Ginsberg

Sometimes I feel in command when I'm writing. When I'm in the heat of some truthful tears, yes. Then, complete command. Other times—most of the time not.

—Allen Ginsberg,
in an interview with Thomas Clark,
Paris Review (Spring 1966)

Louis Ginsberg was a socialist, but his wife, Naomi, belonged to the Communist Party. She was the secretary to a small Communist group in Paterson, New Jersey, where they lived, and when their sons Allen and Eugene (named for the socialist leader Eugene Debs) were young, they twice spent the summer with their mother at a Communist camp in upstate New York.

Naomi Ginsberg suffered from psychotic delusions, insisting that there were wires in her head and that people could hear her thinking. According to Ginsberg's poem "Kaddish," she believed she was "a great woman," "truly a beautiful soul," and that for that reason William Randolph Hearst, Hitler, Franco, the *Daily News,* Mussolini, and many others wanted "to shut me up."[1] Her enemies were, it seemed, mostly fascists and others politically on the right. To say (or even think) what one believed was to suffer.

Communism in America in the 1930s, according to Malcolm Cowley, was a "crusading religion,"[2] and politics on the far left were conducted with great seriousness. As Ginsberg wrote in "A Poem on America," "class consciousness" was imbued "with the appearance of God."[3] The objectives were utopian, and that called for visionaries, but among Americans interested in neither socialism nor communism, there were perhaps relatively few who could distinguish meaningfully between them. Politics meant civilized elections, a choice between Wilkie and Roosevelt or Roosevelt and Landon.

"I did have this desire to be labor leader people's hero," Allen Ginsberg wrote, "that is, with my Jewish left wing atheist Russian background I even made a vow (not ever to be broken) on the ferryboat when I went to take entrance exam at Columbia, Vow Forever that if I succeeded in the scholarship test and got a chance I would never betray the Ideal—to help the masses in their misery. At the time I was very political and just recovering from Spanish Civil War which obsessed me in Jersey age 11 or 13."[4]

Ginsberg eventually concluded, like Kerouac, that "the Marxist rational interpretation of the psychological situation we saw in America was not sufficiently understanding, delicate, tender, to really apprehend the full evil of American society as far as its psychic effects on ourselves . . . were concerned (*Composed,* 75–76). He wanted a more human politics, but, unlike Kerouac, he did not abandon politics as such. In 1961 he wrote in his journal that his "task as a politician is to dynamite the emotional rockbed of inertia and spiritual deadness that hangs over the cities and makes everybody unconsciously afraid of the cops—."[5] Kerouac's work was rarely political, at least explicitly so; it was left to Ginsberg to show how Kerouac's expressionistic aesthetic could be used for political ends.

Kerouac said in 1957 that "the Beat Generation has no interest in politics, only mysticism, that's their religion."[6]

Understanding the Beats

Nonetheless, "spontaneous bop prosody," as Ginsberg indicated in "Wichita Vortex Sutra" (1966) and other major poems, could have political as well as aesthetic ends. In "Wichita Vortex Sutra," Ginsberg reaffirmed the identification of politics and personal emotion which he had seen at home, particularly in his mother, but there was much more to it than that. His enthusiasm for such dissimilar poets as Walt Whitman and William Blake may be explained in part by the fact that both insisted on politics as an extension of the self—rather than as matters of compromise and concession or as something imposed from without. Ginsberg's enthusiasm for Whitman may have been strengthened by the fact of their shared homosexuality. As a homosexual, Ginsberg was in a position to know very well how oppressive a society could be if one did not conform to accepted patterns of behavior. "Further politics will take place," Ginsberg wrote, "when people seize power over their universe and end the long dependence on an external authority or rhetorical set sociable emotions" (*Journals,* 192).

Louis and Naomi Ginsberg in their differing ideologies also wanted to free people from external authorities, but they desired only another authority, the authority of ideology, in its place. Their politics were learned, and their ideas came from books. For Ginsberg, following Kerouac, the only authority was the authority of the individual. All tyrannies, all ideologies should be swept away by what Ginsberg in "Howl" called "the supernatural extra brilliant intelligent kindness of the soul!"[7]

Louis Ginsberg earned his living as a high school English teacher, but he was also a poet and a respected member of the modernist circle which gathered around Alfred

Kreymborg in the 1920s. Although he was associated with some of the more experimental and innovative writers of his time, his own work was relatively conservative. Much as he was a doctrinaire socialist, so was he a careful student of traditional literary form. The forms and ideas came from others; what mattered was the skill with which they were used. Personal emotion was, in short, shaped by convention.

Conservative poetic elegance appealed to many young academic poets after the war. The surprising thing, in view of Ginsberg's later work, is that he was even briefly among them, yet he began as a traditional poet, duplicating the rhythms and sound of early English poets such as Thomas Wyatt and Andrew Marvell. Imitations of that sort, no matter how well done, risk being simply decorative and clever, particularly if the point has less to do with saying something new than with mastering the form. Ginsberg's earliest attempts at traditional verse are not in print, but several poems written in the late 1940s and early 1950s were collected in *The Gates of Wrath: Rhymed Poems, 1948–1952* (1972). Technically they are very skillful, yet they are also in the strictest sense academic, and to understand what they accomplish, one must have a sense of early English poetry. Ginsberg certainly was indebted to his father for that, but it is also true that poetry was formerly more widely studied in high schools than it is now, and readers simply knew more about conventions of English prosody. Nonetheless, the audience which might hear and be pleased with *The Gates of Wrath* was already small.

> Take the skin that hoods this truth
> If his age would wear my youth.[8]

Lines like these from "Complaint of the Skeleton to Time" have their origin in part in the delicacy of the courtier, admired for precision of manner and gesture as well as the capacity to evoke matters that ordinarily would not be discussed publicly. It is a posture that Ginsberg would rarely adopt in later work and then only with irony and humor. *The Gates of Wrath* also includes sonnets written after he first read Kerouac's *The Town and the City,* and they can be seen as ambitious early attempts to reach the high apocalyptic and prophetic mode he developed in 1955 in "Howl" ("City of horrors, New York so much like Hell, / How soon thou shalt be city-without-name" ["Two Sonnets," *GW,* 3]). In "Howl" apocalyptic gestures would merge with surreal humor to create the poem's characteristic tone ("who thought they were only mad when Baltimore gleamed in the supernatural ecstasy" [*Howl,* 11]), but this rarely happens in *The Gates of Wrath.* There is in fact little humor in these early poems, although it is prominent in, for example, "Pull My Daisy," "Bop Lyrics," and the comic self-portrait (using the name Kerouac had chosen for him in *The Town and the City*), "Sweet Levinsky."

The poems are less interesting, however, for their technical competence and their experimentation with tones and moods than for their subject matter and what they suggest about the author's shifting sense of what his own poetry might become. Ginsberg was trying at this time, with very little success, to find a way of making poems from the kind of experiences he, Kerouac, and Burroughs shared. Kerouac was imitating Wolfe, and Burroughs was imitating Hammett. Both had found stylistic models which were in some accord with the hipster world they were trying to evoke. Ginsberg, it is true, turned to the rhythmically complex Thomas Wyatt rather than the more courtly Henry Howard, the ironic Andrew Marvell rather than the formally elegant John Dryden, and the visionary William Blake rather than the skeptical Lord Byron, but he was still locked in a tyranny of formal expectations. He needed a tradition from which to borrow, and the one he chose used formal patterns. He turned, it is true, to the less conventional, more innovative aspects of that tradition, but he was still within a tradition that any academic poet would have approved.

One reason for Ginsberg's long servitude to traditional form (and he worked seriously in that mode for more than a decade) may have been the opportunity it gave to contain and transform intense feeling. Several of the early poems such as "A Western Ballad" are lyrical complaints intended to evoke sympathy or pity as redemptive emotions. The poems turn discontent and depression into song and are in that way cathartic. Expressionism advocates direct statement of feeling rather its formal transformation, and when Ginsberg abandoned the formalist tradition, his poems acquired the power and conviction for which he is known. But even when he worked in traditional form, he searched for ways in which authentic feeling could at least approach, if not be identical with, the surface of the work.

A case in point is his interest in Bedlam ballads or mad songs from the seventeenth century. He found that, "very interestingly, the stanza form that Jack and I concocted for pull my daisy, without knowin the Bedlam ballads, was almost exactly the same."[9] Ginsberg told Neal Cassady that these poems "parallel in many ways my own, the essential

sexual yearning theme plus pull my daisy language so sil-
imare that I feel as if I have reincarnated the old Tom in a
new setting: the difference between mine and the elder being in images of the times, now old Tom wandering on the
RR. and by docks'' (*As Ever*, 94).

Underlying this statement is the assumption that certain rhythms and forms of poetic expression may be adequate to different eras; only the vocabulary and images
alter. Indeed those rhythms and forms (and perhaps in some
way even the language) may be *essential* to an emotion (or
emotional complex) or at least to its expression. That assumption points to a Platonic sensibility at odds with a
Marxist dynamic view of history. Ginsberg is not suggesting here simply that poems involve a fusion of traditional
form and personal content, but that there are certain essentially ahistorical poetic forms which the writer will ''naturally'' evoke in different periods. It is a very conservative
view and one which would encourage a continued investi-
gation of conventional poetics.

It is not only a conservative but also a transcendental
view, and Ginsberg at this time was clearly looking for
some means of transcendence, some way out of his own
miseries and that ''molecular comedown'' which he had
discussed with Kerouac and which found its way into *The
Town and the City*. The hipster, by withdrawing from the
world, implied that its problems were irremediable—or at
least that he had better things with which to be concerned.
The answer was not to change the world but to avoid or to
transcend it. Ginsberg's solution lay at this point not only in
poetry but in mysticism as well, and in the summer of 1948

he experienced a series of visions which were to have a deep effect on his work.

Ginsberg was at that time living in East Harlem, and most of his friends were away from the city. Neal Cassady, with whom he had lived the year before, had written to say that they would not be lovers again. In midst of this solitude and consequent depression, Ginsberg believed that he heard the voice of William Blake speaking his poem "Ah, Sunflower." This was followed by a commanding awareness of the nature of the universe. In Blake's poem, the sunflower, "weary of time," seeks "after that sweet golden clime / Where the traveller's journey is done." Ginsberg identified himself with the flower, escaping time and seeking the ideal, and believed he had been rewarded with a sudden glimpse "into the depths of the universe."[10]

Many years later, Ginsberg referred to the voice he had heard as an "auditory hallucination," but at the time, "my first thought was this was what I was born for, and second thought, never forget—never forget, never renege, never deny. Never deny the voice—no, never *forget* it, don't get lost mentally wandering in other spirit worlds or American or job worlds or advertising worlds or war worlds or earth worlds. But the spirit of the universe was what I was born to realize" (Clark, "Ginsberg," 36, 37).

Other visionary experiences in the next few days seemed to reconfirm that he had been given an authentic revelation, and that in turn provided the motivation for poems which might liberate others into cosmic awareness. The visions did not continue, however, and, Ginsberg said, "I spent about fifteen–twenty years trying to re-create the

Blake experience in my head, and so wasted my time."[11] He turned to drugs—mescaline, yage, nitrous oxide, and others—to induce visionary states, but the Blake experience remained isolated, a moment like that on the ferryboat, which continued to have a profound effect on his work. Just as he would try to reach "the masses" in his poems, so would he reach for moments of Blakean ecstasis and visionary glory. For an epigraph to *The Gates of Wrath,* he chose lines from Blake that suggest absolute conviction that the direction in which he was headed was correct:

> To find the Western path
> Right thro' the Gates of Wrath
> I urge my way;
> Sweet Mercy leads me on:
> With soft Repentant moan
> I see the break of day.
>
> (*GW*, iii)

As technically clever as many of the poems in *The Gates of Wrath* are, they by no means equal their models, and when Ginsberg wrote to William Carlos Williams in 1950 for comment, Williams, Ginsberg recalled, responded abruptly: "In this mode, perfection is basic, and these are not perfect" (*AV,* 139). Ginsberg, in a letter which Williams quoted in *Paterson,* said that he wished "to perfect, renew, transfigure, and make contemporarily real an old style of lyric machinery," but he also felt the need for "some kind of new speech—different at least from what I have been writing down."[12] Certainly Williams, who in *Kora in Hell*

(1920) attacked "Eliot's more exquisite work" for being "rehash, repetition," had little sympathy with poetry that wanted to make "contemporarily real an old style of lyric machinery," and he must have been gratified later to receive a letter addressed not to "Dear Doctor," as the first had been, but "Dear Doc," in which Ginsberg wrote about his work on a labor newspaper in Newark and his ventures into the back parts of Paterson where he had "seen so many things—negroes, gypsies, an incoherent bartender in a taproom overhanging the river."[13] It was obviously in Paterson, rather than *Percy's Reliques* or *The Golden Treasury,* that the new speech could be found.

Ginsberg accepted Williams's criticism and admitted that the "carefulness" required to write the poems in *The Gates of Wrath* had "managed to suppress almost all traces of native sensibility diction concrete fact & personal breath."[14] In his initial letter, he claimed to have "a flair for [Williams's] style," and in 1952 he sent poems which were shaped from passages in his journals and which in texture and sound did indeed have the feel of Williams's work. Williams was impressed and responded with great enthusiasm, saying they should be collected in a book. They were in fact eventually collected in *Empty Mirror: Early Poems* (1961), for which Williams wrote the introduction, in which he said that, like Dante's *Inferno,* the poems were free of "memories of trees and watercourses and clouds and pleasant glades" (*EM,* 5). Things were seen as they were, a modern inferno. This was not a time, said Williams, for the poet to sing sweetly but a time to speak in the language of the newspapers, directly and plainly. Such poems might, to be sure, still embody a "hidden sweetness," but there would be "terror" in the truth they revealed. Ginsberg had accomplished this, and "the craft is flawless" (*EM*, 6).

The earliest poem in *Empty Mirror* is "The Bricklayer's Lunch Hour," originally written in 1947 as a prose sketch describing a young workman at ease during his noon break. Five years later, after receiving Williams's encouraging letter, Ginsberg went back to his journals, found the sketch, and reshaped it as a poem, simply dividing it into lines of approximately equal length and not imposing any syllabic or accentual measure. The result was a simple descriptive statement making no large rhetorical claims and no heightened gestures. It merely presents the scene and concludes that it may soon rain: "and the wind on top of the trees in the / street comes through almost harshly" (*EM*, 31).

Ginsberg is preeminently an elegiac poet. Many of his great works are poems of loss, involving not anger but grief or sorrow and a composed acceptance. "The Bricklayer's Lunch Hour" is not an elegy, but its concluding lines master that contained, objective acceptance found later in such major poems as "Don't Grow Old." In part, of course, this tone results from limiting the poem, as did Williams, to "the actual data of the senses" (*Composed*, 121). Like his mentor, he would insist on "no ideas but in things," and it was the ordinary, the common, both in subject and in diction, that he extracted from his journals.

According to Ginsberg, Williams and such contemporaries as Charles Reznikoff were "working with perceptions that are indistinguishable from the actual perceptions

Ginsberg

of our ordinary mind; but which when recognized, and appreciated consciously, transform the entire feeling of existence to a totally new sympathetic universe" (*Composed*, 151), and in turn this transformation of the actual and the ordinary into poetry became essential principles of Ginsberg's poetics.

Ginsberg at this time also began to experiment with long lines such as he would use in most of his best-known works. "Psalm I" and "Hymn" (both 1949) borrow cadences from the Bible and Blake, and the more frenzied, bop-inspired rhythms of "Howl" are anticipated in "Paterson" (1949): "screaming and dancing in praise of Eternity annihilating the sidewalk, annihilating reality, screaming and dancing against the orchestra in the destructible ballroom of the world" (*EM*, 40).

Empty Mirror also includes "Marijuana Notation," the first of many Ginsberg poems that present drugs as a means to heightened awareness, but, significantly, marijuana is not here an escape into private reveries, which it was (as the poem says) for Baudelaire, but rather a way to a more intense impression of the present moment. The poem ends with a reference to the sound of Christmas carols being sung in the street outside, reinforcing the sense that the drug intensifies awareness of the world beyond the poet's own life.

Reality Sandwiches: 1953–1960 (1963) includes both poems written before *Howl* and poems written after. In Ginsberg's *Collected Poems* (1984), these are divided into two sections, *The Green Automobile (1953–1954)* and *Reality Sandwiches: Europe! Europe! (1957–1959)*. Among

Understanding the Beats

the most significant works in the former is the title poem, addressed to Neal Cassady. When Ginsberg was working on it, he wrote to Cassady saying that he had found "life so unsatisfactory that I am beginning to use my imagination . . . to invent alternatives" (*As Ever*, 147). One of those alternatives is the poem itself, which allows Ginsberg to imagine going to Cassady's home in the West and taking him away from his wife and children for a wild ride through the Rockies to Denver, returning by morning to jobs and respectability. The poem represents a break with Williams's fidelity to "the actual data of the senses" and a new trust in the imagination as such.

Other poems clearly show Williams's influence. "Havana 1953," for example, is a rigorously factual poem that begins "The night café—4 AM / Cuba Libre 20¢: / white tiled squares" and proceeds to sketch, much as Kerouac had done in the opening passages in *Visions of Cody*, what the poet sees at the moment of writing.[15] "On Burroughs' Work" can be read as a prescription for the poetic Ginsberg learned from Williams, insisting on a record of things as they are, with "no symbolic dressing" (*RS*, 40).

Williams's influence is clearest in "Siesta in Xbalba," Ginsberg's most ambitious poem before "Howl." Begun in 1954, " 'Xbalba,' " as Ginsberg said in a letter to the poet John Hollander, "is fragments of mostly prose, written in a Mexican school copybook, over half a year." Ginsberg then reread them, "picking out the purest thoughts, stringing them together, arranging them in lines suitably balanced—mostly measured by the phrase—that is, one phrase a line."[16] Like "The Bricklayer's Lunch Hour" and other works in *Empty Mirror*, "Siesta in Xbalba" is a self-conscious effort to shape journal notations into poetic statement.

Most of the notations at the beginning of the poem involve memories of New York and Ginsberg's visit to the Yucatán peninsula, "where I come with my own mad mind to study / alien hieroglyphs of Eternity" (*RS*, 27). The poem conveys a sense of lethargy and dissipation; it is a meditation or reverie on the past and the need for something new—"an embarkation," "an inner / anterior image / of divinity / beckoning me out / to pilgrimage" (*RS*, 31, 33). In the second half of the poem, "Return to the States," the focus of the reverie shifts from Mayan ruins to mummies at Guanajuato, which suggest what true immortality is. Alone in death, the bodies remind Ginsberg that "the problem is isolation / —there in the grave / or here in oblivion of light" (*RS*, 36). Correspondingly, young people joyful together remind him of the "solitude I've / finally inherited" (*RS*, 37). At the end of the poem, he returns to America with his "few Traditions / metrical, mystical, manly / . . . and certain characteristic flaws" (*RS*, 38). The American which he finds, however, "grinds its arms and dreams / of war" (*RS*, 39).

"Siesta in Xbalba," Ginsberg told Hollander, was "technically no improvement on Williams, except its application of free verse to wordsworthian meditation long-poem—tintern abbey type, or byronic meditation on ruins."[17] But the concluding lines are a distinct advance in Ginsberg's poetry, anticipating the intense political vision in "Howl." The heavily accented rhythms that he would develop in "Howl" are also suggested in another poem written at this time, "My Alba." Those rhythms and the politics of "Siesta in Xbalba" were seeds for "Howl."

Although Ginsberg said that it was probably Williams rather than Kerouac "from whom I got the first touch of a natural prose poetry style," Kerouac's spontaneous method was eventually the greater influence (*AV,* 145). In much of his early poetry Ginsberg remained close to Williams, although phrases like "Christlike subterranean Rimbaud motorcycle Provincetown kicks" in *Visions of Cody* (*VC,* 9), which Ginsberg read in manuscript, seem a likely model for similar constructions in "Howl," where nouns used as adjectives give the lines great solidity and force. But the aesthetic underlying the later poems is Kerouac's "spontaneous bop prosody," summarized in Ginsberg's famous dictum, "First thought best thought."[18]

"The only pattern of value or interest in poetry," Ginsberg wrote, "is the solitary, individual pattern peculiar to the poet's moment & the poem *discovered* in the mind & in the process of writing it out on the page, as notes, transcriptions—reproduced in the fittest accurate form, at the time of composition."[19] Borrowing a phrase from Philip Whalen, he described this sort of poem as a "graph of a mind moving." The "motif and method," he said in his preface to the *Collected Poems,* was "the sequence of thought-forms passing naturally through ordinary mind."[20] The measure used to determine line breaks was correspondingly *"not so much a unit of sound as a unit of thought,"* although "somehow or other the squiggles for the units of sound are identical to the squiggles of thought" (*Composed,* 21). No other supposition about form was necessary or desirable. The poem should be left to find its own manner of expression. As Ginsberg said in another well-known dictum, "Mind is shapely, Art is shapely."[21]

As a "graph of a mind moving," a poem is necessarily autobiographical, and so in his *Collected Poems*, Ginsberg arranged his works chronologically in the order of their composition, permitting the book to "be read as a lifelong poem including history" (*CP*, xxi). He also said, however, "that there is one consciousness that we all share on the highest level, that we are all one Self, actually, that we are all one Self with one being, one consciousness" (*AV*, 5). In turn, "Poetry is the record of individual insights into the secret soul of the individual—and, because all individuals are One in the eyes of their Creator, into the soul of the World."[22] According to this expressionistic assumption, the poet's transcription of the "mind moving" would not be a solipsistic or merely private exercise but would assume a religious significance as testimony or revelation.

As practiced by Ginsberg, it could be political as well. Little of his poetry before 1955 exhibits great political concern. He had abandoned his parents' Marxist beliefs, but under Burroughs's tutelage, he had replaced them with "a sense of Spenglerian history & respect for the 'irrational' or unconscious properties of the soul & disrespect for all Law" ("Prose Contribution," 336). Politics at that point became a struggle between individuals and the institutions and laws to which they were supposed to conform. Watching Huncke trying to survive, Ginsberg said he found his social views "altering increasingly through experience. And I began to get that alienated view of the actual structure of society which everybody then thought was disgraceful."[23]

The problem was that people were not seen as individuals, but as abstractions in a bureaucratized system. "The purely conceptual mind," he said, " . . . had gone mad with the fake conceptions of thinking head cut off from the body and cut off from affective feeling."[24] "Howl" is a direct response to that social reality, epitomized in the poem by the ancient god Moloch, to whom parents sacrifice their children. The first section of "Howl" and part of the third were drafted in San Francisco one day in August, 1955, and the rest followed within the next several weeks. There were extensive revisions, but essentially these only clarified and strengthened intentions suggested in the original draft.[25] Strictly speaking, "Howl" is not an example of "spontaneous bop prosody," but it is very close to this mode and, in any case, very different from the carefully structured poems Ginsberg had been writing until this time.

In 1986 Barry Miles published his annotated facsimile edition of "Howl," prepared with Ginsberg's assistance. Incorporating drafts, and offering footnotes and extensive appendices, Miles's edition looks like a sourcebook for dissertations and scholarly essays—an odd packaging, to say the least, for a poem and a poet who were once poorly served by critics and the academy. In 1957, for example, John Hollander thought the poem "[sponged] on one's toleration" and told readers of *Partisan Review* that as a book, *Howl and Other Poems* (1956) was "very tiresome."[26] Lionel Trilling wrote to Ginsberg heavily criticizing the book and indicating that he much preferred his earlier poems (*Howl: Draft* 156). By 1986, however, "Howl" was commonly included in such standard anthologies as *The Norton Anthology of American Literature*, and

Miles's edition simply confirmed the fact that the poem had achieved a degree of acceptance that would have astonished its critics thirty years earlier.

Miles also demonstrated that, however radical "Howl" looked and sounded to its original audience, it was influenced by a great range of poets, including Christopher Smart, Percy Bysshe Shelley, Guillaume Apollinaire, Kurt Schwitters, Vladimir Mayakovsky, Antonin Artaud, Federico García Lorca, Hart Crane, and William Carlos Williams. To that list, one is tempted to add Whitman, although Ginsberg has insisted that he did not study Whitman closely until later. Ginsberg had, in short, discovered or created a tradition to replace the one inherited from his father and derived largely from seventeenth-century conventions of poetic form.

Miles's edition identifies individuals to whom the poem refers. As interesting as these details are in themselves, their cumulative value lies in reminding readers that "Howl," whatever its associations with the San Francisco Poetry Renaissance, is actually a New York poem, the culmination of Ginsberg's life with Burroughs, Kerouac, Corso, and others in the city's hipster culture a few years earlier. Although "Howl" was written in San Francisco and Berkeley, there are few specific references in the poem to indicate that the author had been west of the Rockies. Nonetheless, the poem is structurally similar to the kind of intensely political, rhythmically driven poem which various San Francisco poets had been writing for more than a decade. A well-known example of this kind of poem is Kenneth Rexroth's "Thou Shalt Not Kill," to which "Howl" may be indebted. Rexroth's poem is, like Ginsberg's, a cry

Understanding the Beats

of outrage against a society which destroys those who do not conform to its desires: "How many are lost in the back wards / Of provincial madhouses?" In both poems Moloch is a symbol of a social and economic system to which society willingly surrenders its young.

Both "Howl" and "Thou Shalt Not Kill" are angry and polemical, but Rexroth's poem, unlike Ginsberg's, is single-minded and humorless, which indeed is the source of its power. "Thou Shalt Not Kill" hammers its message in simple outrage and is very effective because of that. "Howl" is a poem of outrage, too, but its emotional field is more complex. It veers at times into deep sadness, surreal humor, and intimations of joy. The poem's energy is felt indeed in the rapid movement from one extreme emotion or image to another: "who vanished into nowhere Zen New Jersey leaving a trail of ambiguous picture postcards of Atlantic City Hall" (*Howl*, 10). The result is a tangled set of emotions held together by various formal devices, notably anaphora and strong rhythms, which prevent the poem from dissolving into chaos.

Rexroth has no answers, but at the same time, there is no sense of defeat, and one feels that answers are still possible. Ginsberg, on the other hand, expresses the anger of the hipster who knows that there is no escape and that America will simply continue to torment those who refuse to conform. "Recent history," Ginsberg said in the late 1950s, "is the record of a vast conspiracy to impose one level of mechanical consciousness on mankind and exterminate all manifestations of that unique part of human sentience, identical in all men, which the individual shares with his Creator" ("Poetry, Violence," 331). By definition, those who do not share that consciousness are considered mad, but like Artaud, Ginsberg's heroes would rather be thought mad than do what is expected.[27]

Madness in "Howl" is a sign of salvation—a sign that one has escaped "mechanical consciousness," and the poem's ecstatic dithyrambic rhythms seemed intended to exorcise the calmly measured, repressed America that "Howl" attacks. The poem is held together with intense syncopated rhythms, derived particularly, as Ginsberg noted in *Composed on the Tongue* (p. 43), from saxophonist Lester Young's "Lester Leaps In." These drive the lines forward in a powerful, almost frenzied course.

Ginsberg said he "tried to keep the language sufficiently dense in one way or another—use of primitive naive grammar (expelled for crazy), elimination of prosey articles & syntactical sawdust, juxtaposition of cubist style images, or hot rhythm."[28] Of various means used to achieve "density," perhaps the most imporatant, aside from rhythm, is juxtaposition. In the following line, for example, seemingly incongruous images are fused to establish a reality very different from that which would have been suggested by the images alone: "who bared their brains to Heaven under the El and saw Mohammedan angels staggering on tenement roofs illuminated" (*Howl*, 9).

Heaven and the El, angels and tenement roofs: the poem repeatedly draws on oppositions such as these, perhaps the most famous of which is "hydrogen jukebox" (*Howl*, 10). That sort of construction may have originally been suggested to Ginsberg in a study he made of Cézanne's paintings and later discussed with Thomas Clark in an interview for *Paris Review*. Looking for a new way to construct his works, Cézanne discovered how to build them out of contrasts in color, form, and brushstrokes rather than from a conventional perspective. In one of Cézanne's letters, Ginsberg found a statement to the effect that this new method allowed the artist to "*reconstitute* the *petites sensations* that I get from nature" and that, in turn, this "*petite sensation* is nothing other than *pater omnipotens aeterna* [sic] *deus.*" That "petite sensation" was what contrasts on the canvas revealed—or so Ginsberg believed. As he told Clark, he could juxtapose words as Cézanne juxtaposed colors, and in the process reveal "a gap . . . which the mind would fill in with the sensation of existence" (Clark, "Ginsberg," 28, 29).

Later Ginsberg realized that the Japanese verse form known as haiku worked similarly, opening sudden insights into the nature of reality. He also realized that Pound, influenced by Ernest Fenollosa, had achieved parallel effects through his ideogramic method. Fenollosa discovered that Eastern poets juxtaposed two events or observations to imply a relationship or insight which could not be separately stated. In Lazlo Géfin's words, "the juxtaposed 'material' images imply 'immaterial' relationships."[29] Similar discoveries had been made by the Russian director Sergei Eisenstein, who showed in his theories of montage that meaning in films depended on the juxtaposition of images. Collage, of course, operates on similar principles. In all cases, the juxtaposition involves ellipsis—a pause or space between images in which something not literally shown or said is revealed. According to "Howl," "the alchemy of the use of the ellipse" permists "incarnate gaps in Time &

Space through images juxtaposed" (*Howl*, 16). Thus the juxtapositions in "Mohammedan angels staggering on tenement roofs illuminated" evoke possibilities of transcendence and angelic illumination even in the spiritually impoverished American city.

But any explanation, of course, deadens the power of the line. The poet must never state, in Ginsberg's words, the "relations themselves, just the images" (*Journals*, 95). The effect is then direct, immediate—emotional as well as conceptual. "It is a visceral approach to poetry," Paul Portugés has written, "in which the mind rejects its own rational sensibility and undergoes a kind of organic alteration."[30]

In "Howl" the juxtapositions, like the rhythms, are generally violent. Much of the surreal quality of the poem derives from these extreme contrasts, giving it an obvious political force and suggesting regions of awareness that are not open to strict analysis or explanation. These contrasts reveal feelings and mysteries beyond logic and thereby call into question a civilization which claims to value rational, pragmatic procedures.

At the center of the poem is a relationship which the poet imagines between himself and the writer Carl Solomon, to whom "Howl" is dedicated. When the poem was written, Solomon was a patient in a mental hospital in New York—a prisoner, in a sense, of the social oppression and institutions "Howl" condemns. Discussing his reasons for dedicating the poem to Solomon, Ginsberg said that he saw "Howl" as "a gesture of wild solidarity" (*Howl: Draft* 111), and that is exactly what it is, bringing together

the two men in an apocalyptic vision of the loved one walking "dripping from a sea-journey on the highway across
America in tears to the door of my cottage in the Western
night" (*Howl,* 20). The relation between these two men is,
on the larger scale, only one instance of the principle that
unites words like "hydrogen" and "jukebox." Differences
dissolve, and transcendence is revealed.

"Howl" was published in 1956 in a book with several
other poems written about the same time. *Howl and Other
Poems,* Ginsberg said, was "a series of experiments with
the formal organization of the long line" ("Notes for
Howl," 319). In a letter to John Hollander, he expanded on
this, noting, for example, that "A Supermarket in California," "since it's almost prose," was "cast in form of prose
paragraphs" and that "America" was "an attempt to make
combinations of short and long lines, very long lines and
very short lines." The book, in other words, was organized
according to abstract questions of form rather than political
or personal matters and was to be read by poets as an ex-
ploration of metrical and structural possibilities. "Transcription of Organ Music," Ginsberg insisted to Hollander,
involved "a definite experiment in FORM FORM FORM
and not a ridiculous idea of what form *should* be like."[31]

When Ginsberg prepared his *Collected Poems,* he dissolved the structure of the book and rearranged the poems
chronologically in the order written. The change was a crucial one, reflecting a very different sense of priorities.
Empty Mirror and *The Gates of Wrath* were designed, like
Howl and Other Poems, with attention to formal considerations. In the 1950s, when the New Criticism dominated
literary studies, questions of form were more important

than those of personality (which, of course, was one of the principal grounds on which critics attacked Kerouac). But Ginsberg had in fact never been concerned merely with formal experimentation. "Any poem I write that I have written before, in which I don't discover something new (psychically) and maybe formally," he insisted shortly after *Howl and Other Poems* was published, "is a waste of time, it's not living."[32]

Psychic discovery in a Ginsberg poem often involves moments when his private feelings intersect with public or political matters. "Sather Gate Illumination," for example, may seem at first little more than a series of notations made one day at the entrance to the Berkeley campus. The tone is melancholy and dejected as the poet thinks about his separateness, his distance from others; eventually, however, he realizes that if one can love oneself, a link to others is, ironically, reestablished. The most personal is paradoxically the most universal.

In spite of Ginsberg's belief in an ultimate, Whitmanesque oneness among people, the poems of this period are often characterized by loneliness and a sense of unbridgeable solitude. In "A Supermarket in California," for example, he imagines Whitman "eyeing the grocery boys," but all that the "childless, lovely old grubber" can do is watch, much as he, in turn, is watched by the poet. "Will we walk all night through solitary streets?" Ginsberg asks. At the end, he envisions Whitman, having been ferried across the River Styx, alone as the boat returns to the other shore (*Howl*, 23).

"Dream Record: June 8, 1955" concerns William Burroughs's wife, who had been killed by her husband four years earlier when he aimed his gun at a glass balanced on her head. In the dream, she asks Ginsberg what her husband is doing now, where Kerouac is, and so forth. Then Ginsberg asks her whether, even though she is dead, she can love those who are still alive. At that moment she fades away, and Ginsberg sees only her tombstone, its inscription indecipherable.

Much of Ginsberg's work from this period is melancholy and elegiac, but there are exceptions, moments of sudden ecstatic illumination. In "Sunflower Sutra," the poet sits with Kerouac, watching a sunset near the railroad tracks and thinking "the same thoughts of the soul, bleak and blue and sad-eyed, surrounded by the gnarled steel roots of trees and of machinery." Kerouac points out a sunflower growing nearby, the first Ginsberg has seen. It survives in spite of the ugliness around it. "We're all golden sunflowers inside," Ginsberg concludes, "blessed by our own seed & hairy naked accomplishment-bodies growing into mad black formal sunflowers in the sunset" (*Howl*, 28, 30).

In the late 1950s, Ginsberg tried to recreate the intense bop rhythms and ellipses he had mastered in "Howl." In "The Names," for example, he wrote, "O America what saints given vision are shrouded in junk their elegy a nameless hoodlum elegance leaning against death's military garage."[33] However, the best work from this period ("Back on Times Square, Dreaming of Times Square," "At Apollinaire's Grave," "To Aunt Rose," and so forth) is not intense or angry but elegiac and resigned, culminating in the second great work of Ginsberg's career, "Kaddish," published in *Kaddish and Other Poems: 1958–1960* (1961).

Ginsberg

The real sorrow behind the poems of the late 1950s may have been the death of the poet's mother in June, 1956. When he wrote "Howl," Ginsberg has said, he "used Mr. Solomon's return to the asylum as occasion of a masque on my feelings toward my mother, in itself an ambiguous situation since I had signed the papers giving permission for her lobotomy a few years before" (*Howl: Draft*, 111). When "Howl" was written in the summer and fall of 1955, Naomi Ginsberg was hospitalized at Pilgrim State on Long Island. It was thought, briefly, that she might soon be able to return home, but then suddenly and unexpectedly, she died. At her burial, the prayer known as the Kaddish was not said because there were not enough men in attendance. Jewish law dictates that there be at least ten men (the required *minyan*) for the prayer to be said.

Ginsberg's began working on "Kaddish" in the fall of 1957, but most of the work was done one weekend nearly a year later. Several months of revision followed, and by the fall of 1959, it was complete. It stands with "Howl" and "Wichita Vortex Sutra" as one of his principal works.

"Kaddish" opens with the seemingly offhand statement, "Strange now to think of you," and, without identifying whom the poet is addressing, says that it is now a pleasant winter day in the city, but that the night before he sat up "reading the Kaddish aloud, listening to Ray Charles blues shout blind on the phonograph." The tone abruptly shifts in the third line: "the rhythm the rhythm" (*K*, 7). Ray Charles was able both to express and to contain his own torment by staying within the formal limits of the blues structure and rhythm. Similarly the Kaddish both expresses and contains anguish and grief. The secret is in the rhythm, which imposes a formal frame on what otherwise might deteriorate into uncontrollable agony. The poem finds rhythms which permit the poet to express his grief without being overwhelmed by it.

Instead of using juxtapositions that intensify emotion, "Kaddish" is built, like "Siesta in Xbalba," out of simple notations, most of which are followed by dashes indicating a pause or ellipsis in which memory and sorrow can be understood and absorbed. For example:

> Myself, anyhow, maybe as old as the universe — and I guess
> that dies within us — enough to cancel all that comes —
>   What came is gone forever every time–.
>
>   (*K*, 8–9)

As in the *Odyssey* when Odysseus encounters the shade of his dead mother, in "Kaddish" the poet invokes Naomi, talks with her, and tries to come to terms what is now irrevocable.

By the end of the first section, suffering and grief have been subdued to the poem's stately, elegiac rhythm. The second section concerns Naomi's emotional pain as her son understood it when she was still alive. His attempt to see her as she was is also partial atonement for his anger at her for not having been the mother that in fact she could not be. When he last visited her in the asylum, he found a "small broken woman—the ashen indoor eyes of hospitals, ward grayness on skin—," pleading with her son, "I'm not a bad girl—don't murder me!—I hear the ceiling—I raised two children—" (*K*, 30).

This tortured woman, he realizes, is also the "glorious muse that bore me from the womb, gave suck first mystic life & taught me talk and music, from whose pained head I first took Vision" (*K*, 29).

Naomi is the source, the muse, behind his poems, their anguish as well as "the rhythm the rhythm," that elegiac cadence that absorbs suffering, transforming it into song. The section ends with a passage from her final letter to her son: "the key is in the bars, in the sunlight in the window" (*K*, 31).

The next section is a hymn to death, seen as both "the mother of the universe" and "that remedy all singers dream of" (*K*, 7). Three brief sections follow, the first of which gives further memories and images of Naomi's suffering, but then asserts that she left behind "the key," "the key in the sunlight" that can open the door to the mysteries of Creation. The next section invokes Naomi again and is a final farewell to her. The final section envisions her grave over which "crows shriek in the white sun." That shriek, a repeated "caw caw caw," is the "strange cry of Beings flung up in sky," and the poet's memories and those shrieks are said to be "all Visions of the Lord." The final line alternates "Lord Lord Lord" with the shriek of the crows but ends calling on the Lord (*K*, 36).

Just as the chronological ordering of the *Collected Poems* dissolves the unity of *Howl and Other Poems*, it obscures that fact that "Kaddish" was originally to be read as part of a sequence of elegiac and visionary poems. The earliest of the visionary poems is "Laughing Gas," which recounts Ginsberg's recognition under nitrous oxide that, as he wrote Lawrence Ferlinghetti, "the whole fabric of existence is an illusion."[34]

In the late 1950s and the 1960s, Ginsberg used drugs to induce a visionary awareness such as his Blake experience had provided, but these visions could be terrifying, as reflected in "Mescaline" and "Lysergic Acid." LSD eventually gave Ginsberg beatific visions, which were described in "Wales Visitation," but the earlier experiences in "Lysergic Acid" brought confusion and horror:

> . . . at the far end of the universe the million eyed Spyder that
> hath no name
> spinneth of itself endlessly
> the monster that is no monster approaches with apples, perfume,
> railroads, television, skulls
> a universe that eats and drinks itself.
>
> (*K*, 86)

In "Magic Psalm," which is drawn from experiments with yage, Ginsberg calls on God to make him His prophet. The poet wants to reach into the essence of things, "enter the calm water of the universe" and "sound Thy Creation Forever Unborn" (*K*, 94). The response to that, recorded in "The Reply," is a vision of death, "the faceless Destroyer" (*K*, 97). Here, as in "Kaddish," "the mother of the universe" is death, and in "The End" the poet becomes the prophet or spokesman he asked to be. The Creator, "old Father Fisheye," would speak through the poet: "come Poet . . . eat my word, and taste my mouth in your ear." "I receive all," the Creator says, " . . . I enter the coffin forever" (*K*, 99).

Ginsberg

These drug-induced visions were visions of Hell, and a few years later, Ginsberg began to reject visionary poetry in favor of a poetry very close to his early experiments with Williams's poetics. The first major poetic statement rejecting visionary poetry is "The Change: Kyoto-Tokyo Express," written in 1963, but the crisis which culminates in that poem began much earlier. In the summer of 1960 when he was still writing visionary poems and experimenting with yage, he wrote to Burroughs expressing fear "of some real madness, a Changed Universe permanently changed." Burroughs wrote back, ridiculing the idea of "Normal Consciousness."[35] The following spring, Ginsberg visited Burroughs in Tangiers and found him "cutting [his work] up with a razor as if it weren't no sacred texts at all, just as he was cutting up all known human feeling between us, . . . ; he was cutting up his own consciousness & escaping as far as I can tell outside of anything I could recognize as his previous identity." Burroughs wanted to eradicate "every fixed concept of self, identity, role, ideal, habit & pleasure," including "language itself, *words,* as medium of consciousness" ("Prose Contributions," 51).

Two years later, Ginsberg, now living in India, wrote in his journals that he did not think of visions and truth "as objective & eternal facts, but as plastic projections of the maker & his language." The problem for poetry now was "how do you write poetry about poetry (not as objective abstract subject matter à la Robert Duncan or Pound)—but making use of a radical method eliminating subject matter altogether." He thought that Kerouac in his surrealistic associations and "Record of Mind-flow" had already moved in that direction and that Corso, "Boiling down Elements of Image to Abstract Nub," had done so, too.[36]

The writer's business was to examine the material which had made visions and truths seem absolute: "Language, the prime material itself." Gertrude Stein had explored that territory, he said, and John Ashbery was doing it now. So, too, was Burroughs in his cut-ups, his practice of "random juxtaposition" (*IJ*, 39).

But if Ginsberg was willing to consider visions as "plastic projections of the maker & his language," he still saw poetry as personal expression. He said that "although my own Consciousness has gone beyond the conceptual to non-conceptual episodes of experience," he was "hanging on to habitual humanistic series of autobiographical photographs" in his own work (*IJ*, 39). That aspect of his work, clearly indebted at least in part to Williams's influence, underlies the poem written in March, 1963, on the occasion of Williams's death. The poem is as much a set of notations as the works in *Empty Mirror* are. A major long poem, "Angkor Wat," which was written in Cambodia three months later, also shows Williams's clear influence. Drawn directly from journals, "Angor Wat" traces Ginsberg's response to this strange world of colonial greed and profoundly rooted Buddhist belief. In manner, the poem is much like "Siesta in Xbalba."

Williams's influence appears once again in "The Change: Kyoto-Tokyo Express," the poem in which Ginsberg chooses "what Is" over Blakean visions: "This is my spirit and / physical shape I inhabit."[37] The poem is based on a sudden illumination or understanding which occurred while he was riding on the train from Kyoto to Tokyo. Of that experience, Ginsberg said that he realized that "in order to get back to now, in order to get back to the total awareness of now and contact, sense perception contact with what was going on around me, or direct vision of the moment, now I'd have to give up this continual churning thought process of yearning back to a visionary state" (Clark, "Allen Ginsberg," 51).

It would be another decade until Ginsberg fully abandoned his endeavor to reconstruct his Blakean vision. In some ways, he would never cease to be a visionary poet, but the visions he would seek would permit simply awareness of things as they are rather than transcendence. "I see the function of poetry as a catalyst to visionary states of being," he told William Packard in the early 1970s, but by "visionary" he meant "anything that teaches nature."[38] "Wales Visitation," written in 1967, recording impressions of an experience with LSD, concludes, "What did I notice? Particulars! The / vision of the great One is myriad—" (*PN*, 60).

The poems collected in *Planet News, 1961–1967* (1968) and *The Fall of America: Poems of These States, 1965–1971* (1973) attempt to record that myriad character of reality. Many of the poems in these two books were dictated into a tape recorder, line by line, at the moment they occurred to Ginsberg. Their arrangement on the page, he wrote, "notates the thought-stops, breath-stops, runs of inspiration, changes of mind, startings and stoppings of the car" ("Some Metamorphoses," 349). The poetics here are similar to those in "Angkor Wat" and "Siesta in Xbalba," but the tape recorder gave the process of composition a greater pressure and intensity. Immediate response was required, and the poem could not be "composed." A lesser poet might simply have produced banalities, but Ginsberg's poems have moments of great lucidity, immediacy, and conviction. The best is "Wichita Vortex Sutra."

Wichita was the hometown of the artist Bruce Connor, Michael McClure, and others with whom Ginsberg was associated. Whitman had also been there, and the state of Kansas was associated as well with Carry Nation, the temperance leader who "with an angry smashing ax" had begun "a vortex of hatred" (*PN*, 131). This, the geographic center of the United States, seemed to Ginsberg the center of whatever had gone wrong with the country, culminating in American aggression in Southeast Asia. The poem notes that a few hundred miles away in Independence Missouri, was former president Harry S Truman, who had given orders to drop atomic bombs on Hiroshima and Nagasaki.

"Wichita Vortex Sutra" is a meditation on evil in America. Written spontaneously in Kerouac's manner, the poem is one of few antiwar poems from the Vietnam era which transcends the occasion. The evil behind the war was, according to Ginsberg, a matter of language and could be seen, for example, when a bureaucrat's miscalculation implicating America further in Vietnam was explained away as a "bad guess" or when a deadline in a Nebraska newspaper read, *"Vietnam War Brings Prosperity."* "The war is language," Ginsberg responds:

> language abused
>> for Advertisement,
> language used
> like magic for power on the planet.
>> (*PN*, 119)

Ginsberg

Language misused had spread ''a vortex of hatred''—
a vortex which

> ... murdered my mother
> who died of the communist anticommunist psychosis
>   in the madhouse one decade long ago
> complaining about wires of masscommunication in
>   her head
>   and phantom political voices in the air
>   besmirching her girlish character.
>   (*PN*, 132)

Whether or not one accepts Ginsberg vision of history, the poem is among his most effective. ''Wichita Vortex Sutra'' arises not from logical statement but from conviction, anger, and sorrow, and it is these which are Ginsberg's true subjects. Whether or not Carry Nation in fact began ''a vortex of hatred'' is not really an issue, and it does not matter that Truman's residence near Kansas is certainly less meaningful historically than the poem assumes. It is easy to criticize ''Wichita Vortex Sutra'' for its political and historical assumptions, but if one does that, its intent is misunderstood, and its force is lost. The poem's strength lies in its unity of vision and the conviction which holds its disparate assumptions and accusations together. At a time when newspapers and public officials told less than the truth about what was happening in Southeast Asia, the poem, rather than dissolve into uncertainties and confusion, maintains a powerful assurance that the root cause for the war is not what the politicians claimed but rather an evil, ''a vortex of hatred,'' that pervades the culture. With that conviction, the poem moves in powerful rhythms, and it is easy to see why it was quickly recognized by antiwar groups as an important statement. Most such statements now seem no more than polemics, yet Ginsberg's conviction is so intense that, as an expression of one poet's response to the moment, "Wichita Vortex Sutra" remains as effective as such major war poems as Whitman's "The Wound-Dresser" and Rexroth's "The Phoenix and the Tortoise."

In 1970, Ginsberg met Chögyam Trungpa, a Tibetan Buddhist who had recently arrived in America and who taught a full acceptance of sensual experience as the route to enlightenment. Ginsberg, according to his biographer, was attracted to Trungpa's "emphasis on the 'sacredness' of immediate experience, sexual candor, and absence of censoriousnes"—all of which the Beats themselves had advocated.[39] The two men became close associates, and when Trungpa established Naropa Institute, a Buddhist university in Boulder, Colorado, Ginsberg joined Anne Waldman in forming the Jack Kerouac School of Disembodied Poetics as the school's writing division. He also accepted Trungpa as his guru and formally became a Buddhist. In an interview in 1976, Ginsberg was asked how his work with Trungpa, particularly the practice of meditation, had altered his view of North American or world politics. He responded that he no longer had "a negative fix on the 'fall of America'" but saw "the fatal karmic flaws" in both the country and himself and looked for "some basis for reconstruction of a humanly useful society, based mainly on a less attached, less apocalyptic view."[40]

Ginsberg's answer suggests a temperamental, but not a fundamental, change in his political vision. That in fact re-

mained essentially as in "Siesta in Xbalba" and "Howl."
"Plutonian Ode" (1978), for example, begins in a stern
Miltonic voice ("What new element before us unborn in
nature?") and draws on classical, Buddhist, and gnostic
myths in a dithyrambic chant intended to preserve life in the
face of possible man-made apocalypse:

> Take this wheel of syllables in hand, these vowels and
> consonants to breath's end
> take this inhalation of black poison to your heart,
> breathe out
> this blessing from your breast on our creation.[41]

Another political work from this period is "Capitol
Air" (1980), the lyrics for a song which Ginsberg performed at numerous readings in the early 1980s, accompa-
nying himself on the harmonium. The political vision
is fundamentally the same as that in "Howl"—humanity
imprisoned in a police-state: "The moral of this song is
that the world is a horrible place" (*PO*, 107). The individual's solution is to "Trust your heart Don't ride your Paranoia dear / Breathe together with an ordinary mind" (*PO*,
107). One could, in other words, find a wise serenity in
Buddhist meditation—breathing "with an ordinary
mind"—but the object is ultimately not very different from
that sought by "cool" hipsters a generation earlier. In a
world where those who are truly independent are victimized, the answer is to withdraw. If there are solutions to oppression, they are not found by confronting the oppressor
on his own terms.

Many of Ginsberg's other poems in the 1970s and 1980s took as their subject Buddhist meditation and ideas—"Mind Breaths" (1973), "Land O'Lakes, Wisc." (1976), "Do the Meditation Rock" (1981), "Why I Meditate" (1981), and so forth. In terms of their poetics, these works are not an advance over the earlier work but are often conspicuous for their humor and geniality. In "Mugging" (1974), for example, Ginsberg says that, when he was attacked near his home, his muggers overlooked his "shoulder bag with 10,000 dollars full of poetry."[42]

Prominent among Ginsberg's poems from the 1970s are two elegies for his father, "Don't Grow Old," begun in January, 1976, and completed that summer, and a pendant to it, " 'Don't Grow Old,' " written that October. The first begins with Louis Ginsberg's illness ("too tired to take off shoes and black sox" [*MB*, 79]). But the father is utterly pragmatic and not sentimental. In response to lines from Wordsworth's "Ode: Intimations of Immortality from Recollections of Early Childhood" ("trailing clouds of glory do we come / from God, who is our home"), he responds simply, "That's beautiful, but it's not true" (*MB*, 81). He says that when he was a boy he was curious about what was beyond the empty lot behind his house, so one day he walked there and found a glue factory.

In a sense, Ginsberg's father is telling his son the same thing Williams did—not to look for visions but to accept reality as it is. The poet knows that in the end the same will happen to him that is happening to his father: "What'll happen to my bones? / They'll get mixed up with the stones" (*MB*, 82).

The poem includes a song, "Father Death Blues," of which the next to the last verse insists that "Suffering is what was born" (*MB,* 84).

In the first section of " 'Don't Grow Old,' " Ginsberg remembers the occasion twenty-eight years earlier when he admitted his homosexuality to his astonished father. The second section deals with a visit from Louis's grandson, whom he could not understand: "Tell him to go home soon, I'm too tired" (*PO,* 52).[43] The final section, titled "Resigned," recounts an incident a year earlier when his father suddenly

> . . . fell silent, looking at the floor
> and sighed, head bent heavy
> talking to no one—
> "What can you do . . . ?"
> (*PO*, 53)

Louis Ginsberg in these poems seems a man of great, if sometimes mistaken, ideals, a man who can't change his son or his grandson and who is left in the end powerless and alone, but there is no question that his pragmatism is appropriate. The poems document simply an unalterable reality seen clearly. In presenting his account of his father's last year, Ginsberg follows both Williams's call for a poetry with "no ideas but in things" and the Buddhist ideal of "ordinary mind," permitting no deception. Louis Ginsberg's pragmatism intersects with Trungpa's Buddhism and Williams's poetics in these two elegies. At their core is a recognition much like Kerouac's at Big Sur: namely, there are finally no remedies for suffering aside from spiritual understanding (Catholicism for Kerouac, Buddhism for Ginsberg) and whatever wisdom comes from the acceptance of things as they are.

In "Ode to Failure," written two years after the elegies for his father, Ginsberg examines his own inability to realize his ideals. Louis Ginsberg never saw his socialist paradise, and he could not make his son or his grandson the men he wanted. He could not prevent his own suffering and old age. In "Ode to Failure," Ginsberg writes, "I never got to Heaven, Nirvana, X, Watchamacallit, I never left Earth," and concludes simply, "I never learned to die" (*PO*, 91).

"White Shroud" (1983), the title poem of a volume published in 1986, and "Black Shroud" (1984) are among Ginsberg's important later works. Both are based on dreams, and in the first, the poet finds himself in the Bronx as it was when he was a young man. He is, however, older now, yet the family he once knew seems all here again. Looking for a place to live, he passes an elderly lady, who, on closer inspection, proves to be Naomi, and he realizes that now he could live with her:

> Those years unsettled—were over now, here I could live
> forever, here have a home, with Naomi, at long last,
> at long long last, my search was ended in this pleasant way,
> time to care for her before death . . . . [44]

His mother is "content," and he wakes and writes "this tale of long lost joy, to have seen my mother again!" (*WS*, 50).

In "Black Shroud," however, he dreams of his mother

> ... stiff in hypertension, rigor mortis
> convulsed her living body while she screamed
> at the doctor and apartment house we inhabited.
> *(WS,* 69)

Holding her over the sink, he cuts off her head, then looks at it "tranquil in life's last moments" *(WS,* 69). He realizes that lawyers might save him from punishment, but he confesses to the murder and then wakes up. The joy in "White Shroud" is erased by this poem, which returns memories of Naomi to the violence and horror of "Kaddish."

In "Things I Don't Know," the final poem in *White Shroud,* Ginsberg asks rhetorically, "What kind of government ever worked?" *(WS,* 85). The resignation in that question is also found in "May Days 1988," which shows Ginsberg, like Williams, still a master of precise observation:

Should I get up right now, crosslegged scribbling Journals
with motor roar downstairs in the street, stolen autos being
   doctored at the curb
   or pull the covers over achy bones? How many years
   awake or sleepy
How many mornings to be or not to be? [45]

The tone is fundamentally meditative, the poet contemplating his own inevitable annihilation as he had once considered his mother's and his father's. The poem begins, "As I cross my kitchen floor the thought of Death returns," and continues by mixing everyday observations with intense feelings ("May Days," 47). Poetry, Ginsberg said, is "the articulation of different modalities of consciousness,"[46] and, as is the case throughout his work, that is what is involved here: a sequence of insights, moments of understanding. The poet does not offer merely a series of personal complaints or confessions, however; his anguish, he asserts, belong to "Humans & Whales screaming in despair from Empire State Building top to Arctic Ocean bottom" ("May Days," 49). Behind that recognition is, of course, the expressionist's assumption that, in the words of McClure noted earlier, "the way to the universal [is] by means of the most intensely personal." "May Days 1988," like Ginsberg's other important works, begins with the knowledge that suffering is unexceptional, and that it is the business of the poem to record this fact and not become a diversion or the illusion of cure.

Notes

1. Allen Ginsberg, *Kaddish and Other Poems* (San Francisco: City Lights, 1961) 26. Subsequent references are given parenthetically in the text.

2. Malcolm Cowley, *The Dream of the Golden Mountains: Remembering the 1930s* (New York: Viking, 1980) 42.

3. Allen Ginsberg, *Empty Mirror: Early Poems* (New York: Totem/Corinth, 1961) 30. Subsequent references are given parenthetically in the text.

Ginsberg

4. Allen Ginsberg, "Prose Contribution to Cuban Revolution," *The Poetics of the New American Poetry*, ed. Donald Allen and Warren Tallman (New York: Grove, 1973) 321. Subsequent references are given parenthetically in the text.

5. Allen Ginsberg, *Journals: Early Fifties, Early Sixties*, ed Gordon Ball (New York: Grove, 1977) 192. Subsequent references are given parenthetically in the text.

6. Jerome Beatty, Jr., "Trade Winds," *Saturday Review* (28 September 1957): 6.

7. Allen Ginsberg, *Howl and Other Poems* (San Francisco: City Lights, 1956) 22. Subsequent references are given parenthetically in the text.

8. Allen Ginsberg, *The Gates of Wrath: Rhymed Poems: 1948–1952* (Bolinas, CA: Grey Fox, 1972) 19. Subsequent references are given parenthetically in the text.

9. Allen Ginsberg and Neal Cassady, *As Ever: The Collected Correspondence*, ed. Barry Gifford (Berkeley, CA: Creative Arts, 1977) 100. Subsequent references are given parenthetically in the text.

10. Thomas Clark, "Allen Ginsberg: An Interview," *Paris Review*, 37 (Spring 1966): 37. Subsequent references are given parenthetically in the text.

11. Allen Ginsberg, *Allen Verbatim: Lectures on Poetry, Politics, Consciousness*, ed. Gordon Ball (New York: McGraw-Hill, 1974) 18. Subsequent references are given parenthetically in the text.

12. William Carlos Williams, *Paterson* (New York: New Directions, 1963) 174.

13. William Carlos Williams, *Kora in Hell*, in *Imaginations*, ed. Webster Schott (New York: New Directions, 1970) 24; Williams, *Paterson*, 194.

14. Allen Ginsberg, "Some Metamorphoses of Personal Prosody," *The Poetics of the New American Poetry*, ed. Allen and Tallman, 348. Subsequent references are given parenthetically in the text.

15. Allen Ginsberg, *Reality Sandwiches: 1953–60* (San Francisco: City Lights, 1963) 17. Subsequent references are given parenthetically in the text.

16. Jane Kramer, *Allen Ginsberg in America* (New York: Random House, 1969) 164.

17. Kramer, *Ginsberg in America*, 173.

18. Allen Ginsberg, "On Improvised Poetics," *The Poetics of the New American Poetry*, ed. Allen and Tallman, 350.

19. Allen Ginsberg, "When the Mode of the Music Changes the Walls of the City Shake," *The Poetics of the New American Poetry*, ed. Allen and Tallman, 325–26.

20. Allen Ginsberg, *Collected Poems: 1947–1980* (New York: Harper and Row, 1984) xx. Subsequent references are given parenthetically in the text.

21. Allen Ginsberg, "Notes for *Howl and Other Poems*," *The Poetics of the New American Poetry*, ed. Allen and Tallman, 319. Subsequent references are noted in the text.

22. Allen Ginsberg, "Poetry, Violence, and the Trembling Lambs," *The Poetics of the New American Poetry*, ed. Allen and Tallman, 331. Subsequent references are given parenthetically in the text.

23. Kramer, *Ginsberg in America*, 124.

24. James McKenzie, "An Interview with Allen Ginsberg," *Kerouac and the Beats*, ed. Arthur and Kit Knight (New York: Paragon, 1988) 237.

25. The process from draft to final version is traced in Allen Ginsberg, *Howl: Original Draft Facsimile*, ed. Barry Miles (New York: Harper and Row, 1986). Subsequent references are given parenthetically in the text.

26. John Hollander, "Poetry Chronicle, *Partisan Review* 24 (Spring 1957) 297–98.

27. Ginsberg, discussing the opening lines of "Howl," said in an interview, "People who survived and became prosperous in a basically aggressive, warlike society are in a sense destroyed by madness" (John Lofton, "When Worlds Collide," *Harper's Magazine* 280 [January 1990] 13). The "best minds . . . destroyed by madness" were not just the ignored or defeated. It was a double bind: whether one was a success or a failure, one was victimized by the system.

28. Kramer, *Ginsberg in America*, 166–67.

29. Laszlo Géfin, *Ideogram: History of a Poetic Method* (Austin: University of Texas Press, 1982) xii.

30. Paul Portugés, "Allen Ginsberg's Paul Cézanne and the Pater Omnipotens Aeterna Deus," *Contemporary Literature* 21 (Summer 1980) 448.

31. Kramer, *Ginsberg in America*, 169–70.

32. Kramer, *Ginsberg in America*, 173.

33. Allen Ginsberg and Peter Orlovsky, *Straight Heart's Delight: Love Poems and Selected Letters: 1947–1980*, ed. Winston Leyland (San Francisco: Gay Sunshine, 1980) 33.

34. Quoted in Barry Miles, *Ginsberg: A Biography* (New York and London: Simon and Schuster, 1989) 255.

35. William S. Burroughs and Allen Ginsberg, *The Yage Letters* (San Francisco: City Lights, 1963) 55, 59.

36. Allen Ginsberg, *Indian Journals: March 1962–May 1963* (San Francisco: Dave Haselwood/City Lights, 1970) 38–39. Subsequent references are given parenthetically in the text.

37. Allen Ginsberg, *Planet News: 1961–1967* (San Francisco: City Lights, 1968) 60. Subsequent references are given parenthetically in the text.

38. William Packard, "Allen Ginsberg," *The Poet's Craft: Interviews from "The New York Quarterly"* (New York: Paragon, 1987) 44.

39. Miles, *Ginsberg*, 444.

40. Peter Chowka, Interview with Allen Ginsberg, excerpted in *On the Poetry of Allen Ginsberg*, ed. Lewis Hyde (Ann Arbor: University of Michigan Press, 1984) 320.

41. Allen Ginsberg, *Plutonian Ode: Poems 1977–1980* (San Francisco: City Lights, 1982) 16. Subsequent references are given parenthetically in the text.

42. Allen Ginsberg, *Mind Breaths: Poems 1972–1977* (San Francisco: City Lights, 1977) 51. Subsequent references are given parenthetically in the text.

43. These lines may echo Williams's "The Last Words of My English Grandmother," in which the poet's grandmother, in an ambulance on the way to the hospital, asks what the "fuzzy-looking things" are: "Trees? Well I'm tired / of them and rolled her head away."

44. Allen Ginsberg, *White Shroud: Poems 1980–1985* (New York: Harper and Row, 1986) 49. Subsequent references are given parenthetically in the text.

45. Allen Ginsberg, "May Days 1988," *Broadway 2: A Poets and Painters Anthology*, ed. James Schuyler and Charles North (Brooklyn: Hanging Loose, 1989) 48. Subsequent references are given parenthetically in the text.

46. Packard, "Allen Ginsberg," 44.

CHAPTER FOUR

Corso

The poet and poetry are inseparable. You got to dig the poet. Otherwise the poetry sucks.

—Gregory Corso,
in an interview with Robert King and John Little collected
in *The Beat Vision*, ed. Arthur and Kit Knight

Allen Ginsberg met Gregory Corso in 1950. Corso had recently been released from Clinton Prison, where for three years he had served a sentence for robbery and according to a note in Corso's second volume, *Gasoline*, had read his way through "books of illumination."[1]

Corso knew more about life on the street than the other Beats did. Burroughs, Kerouac, and Ginsberg were from middle- or lower-middle-class homes, but he had seen intimately the world of derelicts and thieves that the others watched from cafeteria windows on Times Square. They had read Spengler and Nietzsche and knew from such friends as Huncke and Garver what the underside of American life was like, but Corso spent most of his childhood and adolescence in foster homes and prisons. He was, like Cassady, a survivor, and as Kerouac described him in the character of Raphael Urso in *Desolation Angels*, he also had "a great mellifluous mind, deep, with amazing images"(*DA*, 249).

The other Beats learned the hipster's code of values, but these were Corso's by necessity. Abandoned by his mother and then turned over to foster parents by his father, he learned firsthand the hipster's streetwise sense that no

one, no institution, is really disinterested and that finally
the only reliable place to turn is oneself.

Corso's poetry, as a result, is deeply personal—so
much so as to be at times hermetic and obscure. It takes
more from Poe than Whitman, and at least at the beginning
was influenced by André Breton and surrealism. Poe and
Breton's focus on dreams and the subconscious led Corso
to a poetry similar to what Kerouac and Ginsberg found in
expressionism. Corso has written spontaneous works, notably "Elegiac Feelings American," but generally his poetry, like Poe's, is the product of careful revision and craft.
Poe, as he wrote in a poem entitled "After Reading 'In the
Cleaning,' " is for him the "only American poet."[2] "I
don't think I could let things go without a change," he told
an interviewer, adding elsewhere that "revision is where
you really find out how skillful you are. You have to be like
a magician."[3] Nonetheless, Corso's poems are never
merely imitative; they are "spontaneous, literally," he has
said, but in a statement that might be understood as an extension or refinement of Kerouac's technique, he also
pointed out that "spontaneous poetry is also spontaneous
change when you're working on it." Corso's poetry "insists that its own process, its own fragmentary ritual," in
Richard Howard's words, " . . . is *all that there is*."[4]

Corso, who was born in New York in 1930, never went
beyond the sixth grade, but he developed a private visionary and imaginative world which may have helped to cul-
tivate the facility for startling images which marks much of
his poetry.[5] When Corso was eleven, he lived with his father again, but the next year he was living on the streets and
broke into a restaurant to get food. As he was leaving, he

was arrested and sent to the Tombs, the New York City prison, where "they abused me terribly, and I was indeed like an angel then because when they stole my food and beat me up and threw pee in my cell, I, the next day would come out and tell them my beautiful dream about a floating girl who landed before a deep pit and just stared."[6]

When he was thirteen, he ran away from home. Looking for a place to sleep, he broke into a building and was arrested and sent back to the Tombs for four months. The next two or three years were spent largely in homes for boys. He was then arrested for his part in a robbery using walkie-talkies to warn when the police were coming. The judge, Corso recalled in an interview, decided that he "was a menace to society because [he] had put crime on a scientific basis" and sentenced him to Clinton Prison for three years.[7]

Before his arrest, Corso had written his first poem, "Sea Chanty," in which the speaker says that his mother was eaten by the sea when she did not heed his warning not to hate "the sea, / my sea especially." He found on the shore an unusual kind of food, which the sea told him he could eat. When he asked what it was, he was told that it was his mother's feet. As one might guess, Corso had already been reading surrealist poetry, particularly André Breton's, and it would have a major effect on his work, although he insisted it was "just another toy to play with."[8]

In prison, Corso read his books given to him, he commented, by "angels . . . , from all the cells surrounding me" (*G*, 4). He read a 1905 dictionary and "for three lucky years . . . just got that whole book in me, all the obsolete and archaic words." He read the English romantics, Stendhal, Dostoevsky, and Hugo, but "the one who really turned me on," he said, "was Shelley, not too much his poetry, but his life." Gregory Stephenson, who is responsible for the only extended study of Corso's work to date, has pointed out that "Corso shares with Shelley a zeal for liberty and . . . passionate faith in humankind." Stylistically, however, he learned more from the Surrealists, Randall Jarrell, and, somewhat later, Kerouac. "I don't owe respect to nobody," Corso said in an interview, " 'cause all I learned I learned on my ownsome. Although I did learn from humankind, it was myself and humankind; ergo I have added to it."[9]

In 1954 Corso lived near Harvard, "met lots of wild young brilliant people who were talking about Hegel and Kierkegaard," and was published in the *Harvard Advocate*.[10] His first book, *The Vestal Lady on Brattle and Other Poems*, was published in Cambridge in 1955 with funds raised by Radcliffe and Harvard students. He sent a copy to Randall Jarrell, who responded warmly and invited him to visit.

Jarrell was the poetry consultant at the Library of Congress. He had studied with John Crowe Ransom, had written for *Partisan Review* and the *Kenyon Review*, and was associated with Delmore Schwartz, Robert Lowell, and John Berryman. His work was representative of that which in a few years would be stigmatized as "academic," but his poetic interests as a critic were not narrow or elitist, and he served Corso much as Williams served Ginsberg. Jarrell's work showed Corso how to write poems in terms of specifics rather than general ideas or emotions. Asked by an interviewer where he had learned about poetry, Corso

named Jarrell, who "made me see things around me—fat
ladies at the supermarket. Look at that, he says. What? you
say, because you don't see anything great about them. But
then suddenly you do! He illuminated me this way, got me
to see."[11]

Jarrell may have shown Corso far more. Much of Jarrell's poetry is concerned with innocence and youth in a
world of war and death. In these poems, young men who
wish no one harm are trapped in situations where survival
means being decisive and cruel. In *The Vestal Lady on
Brattle*, as Gregory Stephenson says, Corso "wants us to
look at our society and our lives with the eye of a child."
The subject matter is often terrifying, but it is seen with a
child's clear vision and innocence. The title poem concerns
an aged woman who each morning creates a child, drowns
him, and then "drinks" his body. In "12 Ash St. Place,"
an old man drips colors from his hands. The poet stops to
talk to him and is friendly, but the old man drips "a purple
color on [his] hand" and it burns.[12]

The poems in *The Vestal Lady on Brattle* return repeatedly to thoughts and images of death. "Greenwich Village
Suicide" concerns a woman and whose face is covered with
a copy of the *Daily News* (*VL*, 5). The speaker in "In the
Morgue" is dead and watches two gangsters laid out near
him. Several of the poems, like "Sea Chanty," suggest hatred or fear of mothers. In "Dialogues from Children's Observation Ward," a mother visits her child but doesn't say
hello to him. According to "In My Beautiful . . . And
Things," the speaker will share his "beautiful things" with
a woman if she is "not like a mother or a bitch" (*VL*, 16).

Corso

The principal motif of the poems in *The Vestal Lady on Brattle*, according to Stephenson, "is that of a predatory devouring or destruction of innocence and beauty."[13] But if the world in this book is largely ugly and cruel, the poet has his work and, as he adds in "Cambridge, First Impressions," his dreams. There are no visions out on Cambridge's "Revolutionary Road," but he can leave that and turn, alone,

> ... to books to cans of beer to past loves.
> And from these gather enough dream
> to sneak out the back door.
>
> *(CVL, 35)*

Although the subjects and images in the poems are frequently macabre and frightening, their tone is not. Poetry, commented Corso in a statement quoted at the beginning of *Gasoline*, "comes . . . from a dark river within" (*G*, 4), but an innocent tone transforms it into poems that on the surface are playful and clever. The images are often more startling than terrifying. The poet shows himself and his readers extraordinary things but will not be defeated by nightmares and is always "[sneaking] out the back door." In this sense, the poems, are redemptive; they do not deny the dark river but they deflect it from destructive ends. "The creative artist," as Stephenson writes, "is the embodiment of heroic resistance to the ravening, repressive forces of death and negativity."[14]

In the introduction to Corso's second book, *Gasoline* (1958), Ginsberg said that Corso "wants a surface hilarious with ellipses, jumps of the strangest phrasing picked off the streets of his mind like 'mad children of soda caps' '' (*G*, 7). [15] The language in *Gasoline* is in fact kinetic and delightful, although the poems propose a world one would never want to enter. There is a nightmare just on the other side of the words, and it is the words alone which keep it from breaking through. If one is distracted from the intricate phrasing, one is alone and helpless in that "dark river." "In the Fleeting Hand of Time" for example, evokes a childhood abandoned to "all too real Mafia streets," where desperation ends with the desire to be thrown "beneath your humanity of cars" and with the poet abandoning his "lyre of Orphic futility." The suicide, who has "betrayed" poetry and life returns to the paradise from which he originally came, but once there, he is simply led back "into conditional life" (*G*, 15).

Perhaps the best-known poem in the book is "Birthplace Revisited," in which the poet decides to return to the apartment where he was born, but on his way up the stairs sees "Dirty Ears" with a knife and "[pumps] him full of lost watches" (*G*, 31). There are many other startling images and bizarre juxtapositions here. In "This Was My Meal," a child says that his father "ate my birthday," that the cow brains at dinner look like snow (*G*, 43). In "But I Do Not Need Kindness," the poet talks about a "little old lady," who "rode a spiked car over my head" (*G*, 33–34). Paris, in the poem of that name, is the city of "deathical Notre Dame." It is "Aprilcity," where Baudelaire, Artaud, and other poets now have "worms in hair" (*G*, 48). In "Vision of Rotterdam," that city, repeatedly bombed during the war, "is dying again," but a plan to rebuild it is trapped "amid a madness of coughing bicycles" (*G*, 17). In San Francisco, according to "Ode to Coit Tower," there are "blackjacketed saints . . . Zen potsmokers / Athenians and cocksmen," but

>   . . . not one
> pure Shelleyean dream of let's say hay-
>   like universe
>   golden heap on a wall of fire
> sprinting toward the gauzy eradication of
>   Swindleresque Ink.
>
>   (*G*, 13)

Transcendence in Corso's poetry is found through language and surreal vision. The "pure Shelleyean dream" is a great blaze that could destroy the Swindler writer (such as a counterfeit Shelley like Swinburne?), but it exists only in the poem, transforming dark emotion and nightmare into astonishment. In "2 Weird Happenings in Haarlem," windmills are "spied . . . eating tulips" (*G*, 18), and in "Three," Death spends the day at the movies "when a child dies" (*G*, 39).

Although Shelley is the poet with whom Corso is conventionally associated, he is closer, especially in the early books, to Rimbaud. As Stephenson points out: "Words for [Corso] possess a magical, incantatory power. . . . Like that of Rimbaud, Corso's poetic enterprise is the *alchemy of the word*, the verbal transmutation of the world. His expressive, explosive, explorative utilization of language is at once destructive and constructive, subverting traditional modes of thought and conventional notions of reality, as it exalts desire, freedom and vision."[16]

"I could very precisely see a mosque instead of a factory," Rimbaud said in "Second Delirium: The Alchemy of the Word", "a drum corps of angels, horse carts on the highways of the sky, a drawing room at the bottom of the lake; monsters and mysteries."[17] Similarly in Corso, windmills eat tulips, and the poet sees himself as "the last gangster."

Poe, Corso's "only American poet," is the greater influence, however. In the introduction to *Gasoline*, Ginsberg wrote that Corso wrote "pure abstract poetry, the inside sound of language alone" (*G*, 7). The modern interest in "pure poetry" can be traced to Poe's essay "The Poetic Principle," in which he argued that a poem's objective was aesthetic rather than moral or intellectual. Corso, at least in his early poems, has no interest in judging or analyzing whatever rises from the "dark river." He wants simply the image or observation that is astonishing in itself, such as the American cows on exhibit in the Mexican zoo (*G*, 24).

Some of the poems in *The Happy Birthday of Death* (1960) contain surreal imagery like that in *The Vestal Lady on Brattle* and *Gasoline*. The speaker in "Death," for example, remembers that before he was born, "owls appeared and trains departed."[18] In "Transformation & Escape," God is "a gigantic fly paper," and St. Michael is a sticky material that the poet pastes onto his head (*HBD*, 19). But the better poems in *The Happy Birthday of Death* tend to be more discursive and less imagistic. Corso said that when he first began writing, he thought of poetry as "a concise form, built like a brick acropolis" but decided, after writing the poems in *Gasoline*, that "if I could just go with the rhythm I have within me, my own sound, that that would work, and it worked."[19] The result can be seen here in poems like "Hair," "Marriage," "Power," and "Army."

Of these, "Marriage" is the best known. Corso and Ginsberg gave readings together many times in the late 1950s, and Corso often read "Marriage" as a comic piece to balance the anger in "Howl." The poem begins in the tone of a serious young man contemplating marriage, and the structure is correspondingly formal. The opening line, which hints at iambic pentameter ("Should I get married? Should I be good?"), rhymes with the second. The third and fifth, and the sixth and ninth lines also rhyme, but at that point, the poem abandons any pretense of formality and simultaneously begins to portray weddings and marriage as formal obligations and traps. The poet imagines the priest at the wedding "asking me Do you take this woman for your lawful wedded wife? / And I trembling what to say say Pie Glue!" (*HBD*, 29). Instead of taking "the girl next door" to the movies, the poet would take her "to cemeteries / tell all about werewolf bathtubs and forked clarinets" (*HBD*, 29). At Niagara Falls, he would scream, "I deny honeymoon!" at the hotel clerk and run into the honeymoon suite "yelling Radio belly! Cat shovel!" And back home, he would "[hang] a picture of Rimbaud on the lawnmower" (*HBD*, 30). Nonetheless, although he "can't imagine [himself] married to that pleasant prison dream," he knows that without a wife, he could end "all alone in my furnished room with pee stains on my underwear'' (*HBD*, 32).

The same week that Corso wrote ''Marriage,'' he wrote ''Bomb,'' his other well known poem from the 1950s. ''Bomb,'' which is printed in the shape of a nuclear explosion, is an attempt, in Corso's words, to bring ''all the energy of all the lyric that I could name'' together so as ''to know'' what the bomb is: ''if I start with hating it, with the hate of it, I get no farther than a piece of polemic, a political poem.''[20] The bomb, according to the poem, is the ''Budger of history'' and the ''Brake of time.'' It is inevitable and apparently, like death, morally neutral. When the bomb finally explodes, ''Penguins [will be] plunged against the Sphinx,'' and ''St. Sophia [will be] peeling over Sudan.'' The bomb is the new apocalypse, greater than God: ''thy BOOM His tomb.'' The bomb is declared to be the new master, and the poem ends:

Know that the earth will madonna the Bomb
that in the hearts of men to come more bombs will be born
magisterial bombs wrapped in ermine   all beautiful
and they'll sit plunk on earth's grumpy empires
fierce with moustaches of gold.
(*HBD*, between 32 and 33)

Corso's early poems involve distinct, sharp moments of illumination, but ''Marriage'' and ''Bomb'' and many other works in *The Happy Birthday of Death* are constructions in which subconscious revelation is replaced by politics and social observation. The imagery can be no less startling—as when Corso tells the bomb,

> I want to put a lollipop
> in thy furcal mouth
> A wig of Goldilocks on thy baldy bean
> and have you skip with me Hansel and Gretel
> along the Hollywood screen.
> (*HBD*, between 32 and 33)

Because of their political concerns, the poems are generally less hermetic, their observations and ideas more accessible and less ambiguous, yet their emotional power can be as appalling as the dark rivers that run beneath the surface in *The Vestal Lady on Brattle* and *Gasoline*. As Corso says in "Notes After Blacking Out," "Truth's author itself is nothingness." In a poem, one searches for "the answer," but "Death is knowing the answer" (*HBD*, 11). According to "1959," the final poem in *The Happy Birthday of Death*, "No meaning to life can be found in this holy language" (*HBD*, 90).

Elsewhere, however, Corso's view was less desperate. In the late 1950s, Corso collaborated with Burroughs, Brion Gysin, and Sinclair Beiles in a collection of cut-ups called *Minutes to Go* (1960). When the book was ready for publication, Corso added a note saying that his own poetry "was from the soul and not from the dictionary," and if by doing cut-ups he had seemingly destroyed his own work, it was "poetry I care not for, and so should be cut-up." Burroughs saw words as a form of oppression and wanted cut-ups to dispel their power, but Corso insisted that "you can't destroy language" and that Burroughs would merely "add to it."[21] Corso never published any more cut-ups and had reservations about publishing those in *Minutes to Go*.

Corso's novel *The American Express* (1961) includes a character named Mr. D, "tall and spectral," who, says another, would "unspeak the word and so have done with the human *and* universal predicament."[22] Mr. D. is based on Burroughs during the period of the cut-ups, but the character is not developed, which is unfortunate since Corso lived at that time in the same building as Burroughs, knew him well, and was one of few who could provide an objective description of him as he moved from his early work to his more radical fictions published in the 1960s. The book, which is Corso's only novel, "was written in one month, and it's the one I hate because I really did a fast job on that. It's written so awkwardly."[23] There are comic passages, but the book is not as a whole effective. It was published in Paris in 1961 but has never been published in the United States.

Conceivably Burroughs's destructive intentions in his cut-ups led Corso to reconsider the dark undercurrents in his own work. The poems in his next collection, *Long Live Man*, are, in any case, very different from what he had written before. *The Happy Birthday of Death* ends with "1959," but "Man," the first poem in *Long Live Man* (1962), claims in Whitmanesque lines

That man can *think* soul is a great strange wonderful thing—
In the beginning was the word; man has spoken—
The Jews, the Greeks; chaos groping behind;
Exalted dignity sings. . . .

(*LLM*, 9–10)

"I love poetry," Corso says in "Writ on the Eve of My 32nd Birthday," "because it makes me love / and presents me life," though it also "does tell me my soul has a shadow" (*LLM*, 93). The "dark river" is still there, and "Death," he says in "Writ on the Steps of Puerto Rican Harlem," "remains the same" (*LLM*, 77). The difference is in the way things are seen. If nothing in *Long Live Man* is as strong as the best of the earlier work, the poems can be joyful, celebrating life in ways the others had rarely done.

There were five major books between 1955 and 1962, but between 1962 and *Mindfield*, his collection of "new and selected poems" published in 1989, there were only two. In 1967 Corso said that he had "spent four years thinking, trying to get right back to the source of things. I had this scary feeling that all I know about is writing and poetry, and so I made up my mind to learn." He had gone to Europe, lived in Crete and Greece, and had "read the oldest books—*Gilgamesh*, the Bible, the *Book of the Dead*, all the Greek literature—just trying to put it together for myself."[24]

In Paris he spent six months studying hieroglyphs, and this led to his next major effort, *The Geometric Poem* (1966), not published in the United States until 1970, when it was included in *Elegiac Feelings American*. The poem is important in understanding the transcendental sensibility that runs through Corso's work. According to Stephenson, " 'The Geometric Poem' represents the fullest expression of Corso's fundamental themes of vision and the emancipation of the spirit. In the myths and history of ancient

Egypt the poet discovers a metaphor for the visionary society, and he is inspired to prophesy the coming of a 'perfect Egypt' in which poetic truth and imagination finally triumph over objective reality."[25]

Egyptian civilization survived for four thousand years, longer than any other in history. It was in part a gnostic culture, dependent less on reason than on revelation. As Stephenson points out, "The ancient Egyptians recognized no distinction between the divine realm and the world, all was unity. . . . It is this essential mythos . . . that Corso wishes to revivify. . . . "[26] Geometric forms had mystical as well as logical properties—the line, which seems to have neither beginning nor end, the circle, which is "the highest + purest geometrical form."[27] But nothing in Corso is ever finally triumphant except the dark river, and the poem ends with "3 Prophetic Versions of An Egyptian Downfall." Even this "perfect" civilization is ultimately dissolved.

"Mutation of the Spirit," which was written on heroin in two days in 1964, is in some ways a counterpart to "The Geometric Poem." "Mutation" is in effect a series of gnostic revelations or hermetic texts. Some passages are private illuminations:

> I speak what is demanded of one such as I
> TRUTH ABOVE ALL the demand
> I am a wreck of truth Damn such demand
> I cried I would rather my value be true
> than truth be my value.
>
> (*EFA* , 23)

Others evoke a private, surreal imagery:

Chicken cries Sacramental sobs from the chapel A window
closes
Loneliness grandeur and blue lambs whorled eyes rinsed
light
Swimming deer And now the long hike back to the city.

(*EFA* , 18)

In addition to "Mutation of the Spirit" and "The Geometric Poem," *Elegiac Feelings American* brings together Corso's poetry from the 1960s together with several earlier works ("Spontaneous Requiem for the American Indian" [1958], "Pot" [1957], "The Poor Bustard" [1956], and others) which had not been previously collected in his books.

The hipster's political vision of America as a regimented and repressive society is especially obvious in these poems, but they are also marked by Corso's surreal humor. "I'm afraid to return to America," Corso says in "The American Way":

I am telling you the American way is a hideous monster
eating Christ making Him into Oreos and Dr. Pepper
the sacrament of its foul mouth.

(*EFA.*, 70)

"The American Way" absorbs even those who resist it. The Beats "acquire for themselves their own habits" but

become as distinct and regimented and lost
as the main flow
because the Way has many outlets
like a snake of many tentacles–.

(EFA, 74)

The only answer is "a new consciousness" (*EFA*, 74).
The poem was finished in 1961, and "Mutation of the
Spirit" and "The Geometric Poem" seem to have been
Corso's attempts to reach that "new consciousness." His
elegy for Kerouac, the book's title poem, suggests that
it was Kerouac who had found the alternative and, together with his friends, had become "the very roots themselves" (*EFA*, 4): "We came to announce the human spirit
in the name of beauty and truth," Corso says, and the
proof of Kerouac's success is "the children of flowers"
(*EFA*, 5, 12).

"Columbia U Poesy Reading—1975," collected in
Corso's 1981 book, *Herald of the Autochthonic Spirit*,
is a meditation on the Beats' influence and achievement.
On the one hand, the Beats had the kind of rewards offered
by the very culture they resisted: "the New York Times
paid [Ginsberg] 400 dollars for a poem he wrote about being mugged for 60 dollars."[28] But the poem declares that
Corso, Kerouac, Burroughs, and Ginsberg were "Revolu-
tionaries of the Spirit," who had managed to "boot the
ivory apple-cart of tyrannical values / into illusory oblivion
/ without spilling a drop of blood" (*HAS*, 2). But Corso
then talks about his own involvement with drugs, particularly heroin, as a treason to poetry. At the end he hears

the Muse "moan: 'O Gregorio, Gregorio / you'll fail me I know,' " but his spirit replies, "Not so" (*HAS*, 5). "Columbia U Poesy Reading—1975" is Corso's rededication to poetry.

When the poem was written, Corso was planning a new book to be titled "Who Am I—Who I Am." His only copy of the manuscript was stolen, however, and there were no further books until *Herald of the Autochthonic Spirit* was published in 1981. By then, of course, he could no longer be a young Rimbaud. He had, as he wrote in "Feelings on Getting Older," "entered prison the youngest and left the youngest / of Ginsberg Kerouac Burroughs . . . the youngest," but now he had "vintage eyes" (*HAS*, 52–53). The poems in *Herald of the Autochthonic Spirit* include reflections on youth (such as "What the Child Sees," "Youthful Religious Experiences," and "When a Boy . . . ") and meditations on aging (such as "The Mirror Within," "Getting to the Poem," "How Not to Die"). Among the latter, the best may be "The Whole Mess . . . Almost," in which the poet tells how he threw out of his window "Truth, squealing like a fink," God, Love, Beauty, and other things which had once been important to him. Having second thoughts about Beauty, however, he ran outside in time to catch her before she hit the ground. Then he threw out Death, so that all he had left, beside Beauty, was Humor, to which he could only say, "Out the window with the window!" (*HAS*, 48–49). The dark river, at least here, was gone.

Mindfield: New & Selected Poems (1989) is largely a selection of poems from Corso's earlier books, but it also includes a section of previously unpublished poems including several written since *Herald of the Autochthonic Spirit* (1981). "Poet Talking to Himself in the Mirror" asserts again his essential role as a poet. He says he doesn't have an agent as Ginsberg and Ferlinghetti do, and he wonders if he should get one and make money but then concludes, "No way, Gregory, stay / close to the poem!!!"[29]

"Field Report," the long, rambling poem which follows "Poet Talking to Himself in the Mirror" and with which the volume ends, is a series of reflections and meditations in which Corso reaffirms the importance of poetry and his own position as a poet. The poem is largely discursive and very different from his early hermetic work, but there are still effective metaphors. "Old age," Corso says near the end of the poem,

> . . . comes
> like a stranger cat in the night
> purring its head against your head
> quiet old age . . .
>
> (*M*, 267)

"Field Report" continues Corso's general direction since the 1960s away from the extraordinary surreal imagery for which he was first known. Nonetheless, like his earliest work, it is personal, lyrical, and deeply serious. As he insisted many years earlier, "I, as a poet, am the poetry I write." "After all," he told an interviewer, "I know what I am putting down there and why I am putting it down."[30]

And that is the way Corso's work should be read and understood. The poetics behind the poems are antithetical to any critical position which would discuss the work as separate from its creator. The poems are not confessions, but they are profoundly personal, the expression of the poet's preoccupations and sensibility. In the preface to his *Collected Poems* Ginsberg said that he arranged the volume "in straight chronological order to compose an autobiography" (*CP*, xix), and in effect that is also what Corso did in *Mindfield*.

By its very nature, Corso's poetry denies the validity of formal critical evaluation. The reader or listener is left simply to recognize whether a correspondence exists between his or her experience and the poet's. Richard Howard found the poems plagued with "vulgarities and distractions and boastings" yet manifesting at the same time "the elements of a giant art."[31] Corso, however, would never edit out those "vulgarities and distractions and boastings," for that would suggest that there was an ideal the poet should achieve, while in fact what matters is the record of what the poet already is. To read Corso's poems is to encounter the complexity of the poet himself. "The poet and his poetry," he said, "are inseparable."[32]

Notes

1. Gregory Corso, *Gasoline / The Vestal Lady on Brattle* (San Francisco: City Lights, 1958) 4. Subsequent references are given parenthetically in the text.

2. Gregory Corso, *Long Live Man* (New York: New Directions, 1962) 89. Subsequent references are given parenthetically in the text.

3. Michael Andre, "An Interview with Gregory Corso," *Unmuzzled Ox* 22 (Winter 1981): 157; quoted in Neeli Cherkovski, *Revolutionary of*

Understanding the Beats

the Spirit: Gregory Corso," *Whitman's Wild Children* (Venice and San Francisco: Lapis, 1988) 191.

4. Andre, "Gregory Corso," 157; Robert King and John Little, "I'm Poor Simple Human Bones: Gregory Corso," *The Beat Vision*, ed. Arthur and Kit Knight (New York: Paragon, 1987) 172; Richard Howard, "Gregory Corso," *Alone in America*: *Essays on the Art of Poetry in the United States Since 1950* (New York: Antheneum, 1980) 79.

5. See Gregory Corso, "When I Was Five I Saw a Dying Indian," *Evergreen Review* 48 (August 1967) 29–30, 83–87 for his account of his childhood visionary experiences.

6. Gregory Corso, Biographical Note, *The New American Poetry*, ed. Donald Allen (New York: Grove, 1960) 430.

7. Gavin Selerie, ed., *Riverside Interviews 3: Gregory Corso* (1982) 23.

8. Quoted in Cherkovski, "*Revolutionary of the Spirit*," 181.

9. Andre, "Gregory Corso," 127; King and Little, "Poor Simple Human Bones," 154; Gregory Stephenson, " 'The Arcadian Map': Notes on the Poetry of Gregory Corso," *The Daybreak Boys: Essays on the Literature of the Beat Generation* (Carbondale and Edwardsville: Southern Illinois University Press, 1990) 76; Selerie, ed., *Riverside Interviews*, 41.

10. Corso, Biographical Note, *The New American Poetry*, ed. Allen, 430.

11. Quoted in Bruce Cook, *The Beat Generation* (New York: Scribners, 1971) 144.

12. Gregory Stephenson, *Exiled Angel: A Study of the Work of Gregory Corso* (London: Hearing Eye, 1989) 14; Gregory Corso, *The Vestal Lady on Brattle* (Cambridge, MA: Brukenfeld, 1955) 1, 25. Subsequent references to *The Vestal Lady* are given parenthetically in the text.

13. Stephenson, *Exiled*, 11.

14. Stephenson, *Exiled*, 13.

15. Conceivably Corso acquired his sense of ellipses from Ginsberg, but he could also have derived it from Surrealism.

16. Stephenson, *Exiled*, 30.

17. Arthur Rimbaud, *Complete Works*, trans. Paul Schmidt (New York: Harper and Row, 1975) 205.

18. Gregory Corso, *The Happy Birthday of Death* (New York: New Directions, 1960) 38. Subsequent references are given parenthetically in the text.

19. Andre, "Gregory Corso," 125.

20. Andre, "Gregory Corso," 132.

21. Sinclair Beiles, William Burroughs, Gregory Corso, and Brion Gysin, *Minutes to Go* (Paris: Two Cities, 1960) 63; Andre, "Gregory Corso," 132.

22. Gregory Corso, *The American Express* (Paris: Olympia, 1961) 17, 141.

23. Andre, "Gregory Corso," 128.

24. Cook, *The Beat Generation*, 147.

25. Stephenson, *Exiled*, 65.

26. Stephenson, *Exiled*, 65.

27. Gregory Corso, *Elegiac Feelings American* (New York: New Directions, 1970) 50. Subsequent references are given parenthetically in the text.

28. Gregory Corso, *Herald of the Autochthonic Spirit* (New York: New Directions, 1981) 1. Subsequent references are given parenthetically in the text.

29. Gregory Corso, *Mindfield: New & Selected Poems* (New York: Thunder's Mouth, 1989) 237. Subsequently referred to parenthetically in the text.

30. Gregory Corso, "Some of My Beginning . . . and What I Feel Right Now," *Poets on Poetry*, ed. Howard Nemerov (New York: Basic, 1966) 72; Andre, "Gregory Corso," 140.

31. Howard, "Gregory Corso," 83.

32. Andre, "Gregory Corso," 140.

CHAPTER FIVE

Burroughs

The Word clearly bears the single identifying feature of virus: it is an organism with no internal function other than to replicate itself.

—William S. Burroughs,
"Ten Years and a Billion Dollars," collected in
The Adding Machine

William Burroughs's parents sent him to the Los Alamos Ranch School, a socially respected boys' school in New Mexico, when he was fifteen. In his senior year, he fell in love with a boy who told others about it, and a few weeks before graduation, Burroughs' parents withdrew him from the school. While there, he had kept a diary in which he recorded the things he could not say in public. Back at home in St. Louis, however, the diary seemed weak or simply wrong: it was, he said, "so maudlin, so trite, the emotions expressed seemed so false."[1]

According to the Polish-American linguist Count Alfred Korzybski, emotions and the words used to name and describe them are not equivalent. In *Science and Sanity*, Korzybski pointed out that "generalities without a clear referent are misleading and meaningless." Burroughs thought highly of Korzybski, attended a series of lectures by him in 1939, and felt that *Science and Sanity* "should be required for all college students and for anyone who is concerned with precision of thought and expression."[2]

Like Korzybski, Burroughs is concerned with precise naming. His fiction dismantles meanings and values which

Burroughs

disguise ambitions and less noble ends, and his cut-ups try to dismantle language itself. Kerouac, Ginsberg, and Corso proposed extreme alternatives to what they considered a repressive and conformist culture, but Burroughs's alternative was far more radical—a reconsideration of language and its power in recording and interpreting experience. "I have blown a hole in time . . . ," the narrator says at the end of *Cities of the Red Night.* "Let others step through."[3] Burroughs had tried to do the same, freeing his readers from the past as embodied in language.

Burroughs argued that writing, like other arts, "is magical in origin. That is, it was originally employed for ceremonial purposes to produce very definite effects. In the world of magic nothing happens unless someone wants it to happen, *wills* it to happen, and there are certain magical formulae to channel and direct the will. The artist is trying to make something happen in the mind of the viewer or reader."[4]

When Burroughs was thirteen, his parents moved to the St. Louis suburbs, where they supported themselves with a business named Cobble Stone Gardens, specializing in lawn decorations, garden accessories, and gift items. The business was successful, and the family lived well. After leaving Los Alamos, he attended a private school in St. Louis for a year and, in 1931, entered Harvard. Following his graduation in 1936, he went to Vienna to study medicine but did not complete a degree and returned to the United States the following year. He did graduate work at Harvard and Columbia, and in 1942, he was drafted into the army but was soon discharged for psychological reasons. He worked briefly in Chicago as an exterminator and in 1943 moved to New York, where he began experimenting with drugs, eventually becoming addicted to heroin. Hipster manners and values had their origin largely in the world of junkies and drugs, and Burroughs's addiction gave him an entrée to hipster culture at the moment of its formation.[5]

Two factors are of particular importance to Burroughs's fiction and its view of the world: his homosexuality and his addiction to heroin. Although Burroughs had a son by his common law wife, Joan Vollmer, he was predominantly gay, and homosexuality in the middle years of the century was conventionally seen either as a psychological problem or as a crime. As a homosexual, Burroughs was by definition an outsider, the position from which all his fiction is written. The sexuality in his work is rarely erotic, but it is explicitly homosexual, and if there is any paradise in the fiction, it is occupied exclusively by boys and men.

In the 1940s, drugs were considered perhaps an even greater crime than homosexuality. Huncke has said that Burroughs "became a drug addict principally as a result of research more than anything else."[6] Addiction gave Burroughs a privileged view of human psychology. The addict, he held, did not suffer from a psychological illness. Rather, heroin provided a pleasant experience (at least initially), and anyone, Burroughs argued, would naturally gravitate to what was pleasurable. "Junk," he wrote, "is the ideal product. . . . The client will crawl through a sewer and beg to buy."[7]

The heroin addict was merely an extreme example of a behavioral pattern found everywhere, Burroughs thought.

Burroughs

To be addicted to anything meant to be possessed by some need that does not satisfy itself and that requires one to prey on others. For similar reasons, as Burroughs often pointed out in interviews as well as fictional works, one could become addicted to power or sex. "Junk is a key," he wrote, "a prototype of life. If anyone fully understood junk, he would have some of the secrets of life, the final answers."[8]

Burroughs moved to Texas with Joan Vollmer in 1946 and, two years later, settled in Louisiana. In 1949, he crossed into Mexico to escape drug charges. He lived in Mexico City, where drugs were plentiful, and the following year began his first novel, *Junkie* (or *Junky*, according to the spelling popularized by the publication of the 1977 edition). In 1951 he aimed his gun at a glass balanced on his wife's head, missed, and killed her. He was arrested but released on bail, left Mexico and, eventually settled in Tangiers, where he lived at first in a male brothel. He was addicted to heroin until 1956.

Junky was published as a paperback in 1953 under the pseudonym William Lee. Perhaps to make it seem more respectable, it was published in the same volume as an autobiographical work entitled *Narcotics Agent* by Maurice Helbrant. The book sold very well (more than a hundred thousand copies in the first year), and Burroughs had written a sequel entitled *Queer*, but the publisher was not willing to risk issuing that. It was one thing to publish a book about drugs; it was a very different matter to publish a book about homosexuality. *Junky* talks about the homosexual world in Mexico City, but the subject is secondary to drugs. *Queer* deals explicitly with homosexual relationships, emotions, and fantasies, and, according to Burroughs's

biographer, "the people at A. A. Wyn [the publisher of
Ace Books] decided that publishing *Junky* was dangerous
enough without teaming it with a book . . . that might land
them all in jail."[9]

As a result, *Queer* remained in manuscript for more
than thirty years. Yet these two books should be read together, for they are complementary studies in addiction.
Sexuality is seen as a compulsion much like the need for
drugs. Both addictions emerge in a world divided between
the hunters and the hunted. There is no strong affection between people, only obsessive desires and needs. The central
figure in both novels is William Lee, drawn from Burroughs himself, and episodes in both are largely autobiographical. They share with hard-boiled novels, to which
they are also stylistically indebted, a perception of life
as victimization. The tone tends to be spare, direct, and
matter-of-fact—qualities which Burroughs took from
Dashiell Hammett and Raymond Chandler.

Junky opens with a visit from "a hard-working thief"
to Lee in his "dirty apartment," where "the wallpaper was
flaking off because the radiator leaked steam."[10] The thief
has morphine, which he wants Lee to sell. Eventually Lee
tries the morphine himself. Repeated use leads to addiction, experiments with other drugs, and eventual arrest for
using a false name on a narcotics prescription. Lee meets
other junkies and works with them as a pickpocket, drug
pusher, and so forth to support his habit. Addiction involves both paranoia and need, which leads to an intensification and concentration of experience. The junky and the
pusher see a selective world, but they see it with hallucinatory precision.

Lee goes to the federal narcotics hospital in Kentucky to break his habit, but the cure only lasts a few months. He then goes to New Orleans, where he is again arrested on a narcotics charge and leaves for Mexico to escape prosecution. On the way, he passes through the Rio Grande Valley, which offers a terrifying vision of life without need or desire, the technological paradise that postwar America was creating. The valley is reclaimed desert, "a vast suburb of flimsy houses," "where the new anti-life force is breaking through" (*J*, 105, 106). Mexico City, in contrast, is filled with young hipsters, driven there by a crackdown on drugs in the United States, but they "seem lacking in energy and spontaneous enjoyment of life" (*J*, 147). Paradoxically, in their lethargy and boredom, they are like the suburbanites in the Rio Grande Valley.

In *Junky*, the only important contacts between people involve buying and selling. Otherwise, everyone—the junkies in New York, the farmers in Texas, the hipsters in Mexico—have nothing to do but wait. Lee repeatedly tries to cure himself of addiction, but in the novel's terms, aside from addiction, there can be nothing but waiting. One is "cured," but "then you hit a sag. . . . You don't even want junk. The junk craving is gone, but there isn't anything else" (*J*, 101). In the end, Lee decides to go to Colombia where he can find yage, a powerful drug which he believes "may be the final fix" (*J*, 152).

Junk depresses or eliminates libido, but as Burroughs points out in his introduction to *Queer*, when the habit is broken, sexuality is again as powerful as it had been in adolescence, and having been cured of drugs, Lee finds himself suddenly obsessed with a young man named Allerton.

Homosexuality, says Lee, is "a curse."[11] Although heroin initially provides pleasure, the need becomes metabolic, and similarly, sexual possession becomes a need in itself. Sexual desire in Burroughs's early work rarely involves pleasure; it is a corrosive need that is only momentarily satisfied.

Lee believes in telepathy. If he is to satisfy his need, he must be able to control the men who could serve his ends, and yage, he believes, permits not only telepathic powers but also thought control: "Think of it: thought control," he tells Allerton. "Take anyone apart and rebuild to your taste" (*Q*, 89).

In fact yage proved to be a powerful hallucinatory drug, and Burroughs's experiences with it are recorded in *The Yage Letters*: "The blood and substance of many races . . . [as well as] new races as yet unconceived and unborn, combinations not yet realized passes through your body. Migrations, incredible journeys through deserts and jungles and mountains. . . . The Composite City where all human potentials are spread out in a vast silent market."[12]

The passage goes on to describe such things as a "sluggish river jumping with vicious fish, vast weed-grown parks where boys lie in the grass or play cryptic games. Not a locked door in the City. Anyone comes in your room any time. . . . Hipsters with smooth copper-colored faces lounge in doorways . . . , their faces blank with an insect's unseeing calm" (*YL*, 44). Eventually this vision of a "Composite City" was incorporated into Burroughs's novel *Naked Lunch*, as a description of Interzone. Interzone is generally thought to be based on Tangiers, but Burroughs had not in fact been there before the passage was written.[13] Mexico City, New York, and St. Louis were all, however, in their own ways "composite cities." Interzone began as a hallucination of the modern city where the deviant can find everything he needs except privacy. Yage may not have given Burroughs telepathic powers, but it gave him a starting point for his most famous novel.

All of Burroughs's major fiction is hallucinatory— which is not to say that it is false but that it involves a surrealistic intensification of the ordinary world. He remained one of Korzybski's disciples, but the reality described in his fiction beginning with *Naked Lunch* does not derive from what, in *The Yage Letters*, he called "Normal Consciousness" (*YL*, 59). "There is only one thing a writer can write about," Burroughs said in his "Atrophied Preface" to *Naked Lunch*: "*what is in front of his senses at the moment of writing.* . . . I am a recording instrument" (*NL*, 221, Burroughs's ellipsis). The documentary function of the writer was the same as it had been in *Junky*, but his object became "*Direct* recording of certain areas of psychic process" (*NL*, 221).

Those visions tended to take the form of routines. Burroughs's first work, written in 1938 in collaboration with his friend Kells Elvins, was a routine entitled "Twilight's Last Gleaming," which in abbreviated form eventually found its way into *Nova Express*. The complete routine was published in 1989 in *Interzone*. The setting is a sinking ship, and the characters include a drunken Dr. Benway, who appears frequently in Burroughs's work. Benway is performing an appendectomy at the moment the ship is rocked by an explosion. "Sew her up!" he orders the nurse. "I can't be expected to work under such conditions."[14]

"Routines," Burroughs wrote, "are completely spontaneous and proceed from whatever fragmentary knowledge you have." The writer has certain characters (the mad doctor, the helpful nurse, the unwitting patient), a situation (the operation during the ship's explosion), and little else. There is, as a result, considerable room for improvisation, but that improvisation can never violate assumptions about the characters' psychology. In that way, the routine must be absolutely realistic. As an "art form," said Burroughs, the routine "is not *completely symbolic*; . . . it is subject to shlup over into 'real' action at any time."[15]

Routines are in one sense a literary convention. The porter's monologue in *Macbeth* is a routine. So is the graveyard scene in *Hamlet*. Nineteenth-century American humorists such as Petroleum V. Nasby, Artemus Ward, Josh Billings, and, most important, Mark Twain devised routines and peopled them, as did Burroughs, with extravagant characters speaking in dialect and unwittingly exposing their veniality and conceit. But Burroughs's routines may also have less literary origins. The routine was after all an important and popular component of burlesque and vaudeville shows. Indeed the hospital skit in which a crazy doctor did things like operate with a penknife or a hacksaw was a staple in such shows, and it may very well have been in this context that Dr. Benway was born. In any case, routines in burlesque and vaudeville used comedy to undermine the controlled, settled world of conventional expectations, and it was perhaps for that reason that Beckett used routines to structure *Waiting for Godot*. When conventional expectations are dissolved, as happens there, motivations and desires are suddenly seen with hallucinatory clarity.

The routine may be comic and exhilarating as it exposes motivations and character, but its humor is never comforting because it suggests nothing better to replace the illusions it devastates. "I am subject to continual routines, which tear me apart like a homeless curse," Burroughs wrote when he was working on *Naked Lunch*. "I feel myself drifting further and further out, over a bleak dream landscape of snow-covered mountains."[16]

"Man is least himself when he talks in his own person," Oscar Wilde argued. "Give him a mask and he will tell you the truth."[17] But the mask which is assumed will also determine the kind of truth that can be told. The mask provided by routines allowed Burroughs to say things that the mask of journalistic, hard-boiled prose did not. As long as he was modeling his work on Chandler and Hammett, he had to give an impression of almost journalistic or documentary factuality, but the routine allowed him to speak more freely or at least imaginatively. Because of their hallucinatory quality, routines also permitted Burroughs to convey an intensified sense of the paranoid world of the addict and the homosexual. They allowed Burroughs to reveal fears and hatreds that could only be obliquely suggested by literal narrative. Speaking of the routines in *Queer*, he said they "set one's teeth on edge because of the ugly menace just behind or to one side of them, a presence palpable as a haze" (*Q*, xix).

According to Burroughs, in *Queer* Lee uses the routine as "a frantic attention-getting format," a way of making another man pay attention, but Allerton resists being seduced by this verbal play (*Q*, xv). Eventually Lee's "audience becomes internalized," and he is "pressed into the world of fiction," choosing writing over his life (*Q*, xvi).

Writing from Tangiers in 1956, while *Naked Lunch* was in process, Burroughs told Ginsberg he felt compelled to write only when he was "possessed by routines" (*LAG*, 153). He wanted these routines to cohere as a traditional novel, but early in the writing, he found himself with "pieces of a novel, and the pieces don't fit together" (*LAG*, 76). After his cure from heroin addiction, the work came "like dictation," "practically automatic writing" (*LAG*, 173–74). In Kerouac's *Desolation Angels*, Duluoz asks the Burroughs character, Bull Hubbard, where the material is coming from, and he replies, "from other planets."

In 1958, a section of the book was published in the *Chicago Review*, a student magazine at the University of Chicago. An uproar followed because of obscenities in the piece, and when as a result the university failed to print the next issue of the magazine, a privately funded journal, *Big Table*, was established. The first issue included (in addition to Kerouac's "Old Angel Midnight" and poems by Corso) several routines from *Naked Lunch*. *Big Table* was seen by Maurice Girodias, the owner of the Olympia Press in Paris, who decided that he would be willing to publish the book and insisted on seeing the complete text in two weeks.[18] There was still no particular sequence to the material, and, except for one switch (placing the Hauser and O'Brien section at the end), the routines were published exactly in the haphazard order in which they were prepared for the typesetter. "You can cut into *Naked Lunch* at any intersection point," Burroughs wrote in his "Atrophied Preface" (*NL*,

224). As a result *Naked Lunch* does not have a fixed linear order like a conventional novel but is rather like a globe: start at one point and move randomly and sooner or later you will reach all the other points. Similarly, the book might be compared to a labyrinth leading the reader through twists and curves of narrative and observation, then doubling back and starting over again. It is also like a serial poem in which each part illuminates and is illuminated by every other.

"I feel there is some hideous new force loose in the world like a creeping sickness, spreading, blighting," Burroughs had written in his journal while working on the novel. "Control, bureaucracy, regimentation, these are merely symptoms of a deeper sickness that no political or economic program can touch. What is the sickness itself?" ("Lee's Journal," 69). He concluded that the disease was caused by a "virus" much more pervasive and threatening than the old repressiveness of genteel society. Burroughs had taken the hipster's paranoid ideology and intensified it. "We have a new type of rule now," he wrote. "Not one-man rule, or rule of the aristocracy or plutocracy, but of small groups elevated to positions of absolute power by random pressures, and subject to political and economic factors that leave little room for decision. They are representatives of abstract forces who have reached through power to surrender of self" ("Lee's Journal," 71).

The "real theme" of *Naked Lunch*, Burroughs told Ginsberg, "is Desecration of the Human Image by the control addicts who are putting out the virus" (*LAG*, 195). *Naked Lunch* describes a Pavlovian nightmare, a masterwork of sinister operant conditioning. Behavioral psychology, derived from Pavlov's observation that behavior was conditioned and reflexive, was appropriate to an age which saw Nazis, Stalinists, and Italian and Spanish fascists assume mechanistic control of vast populations while centralization and conformity in the United States increasingly pervaded everything from government to entertainment. Whatever earlier generations had said about the importance of individual will or private emotions, it seemed that the right stimulus, the right word at the right time, overruled any other consideration. Something was destroying in Burroughs's words, "the symbolizing, myth-making, intuitive, empathizing, telepathic faculty in man, so that his behavior can be controlled and predicted by the scientific methods that have proved so useful in the physical sciences" (*LAG*, 88). Whether the underlying cause was identified as a conditioned reflex or seen metaphorically as a drug or a virus, behavior was magically and permanently transformed. Behavioral conditioning, like heroin, seemed effectively metabolic.

According to B. F. Skinner, who was beginning his research at Harvard when Burroughs was an undergraduate, the basic mechanism was simple: "behavior is shaped and maintained by its consequences." That principle underlies the utopia Skinner described in his novel *Walden Two* (1948), but Burroughs's Dr. Benway puts behavioral control to less benevolent ends. Benway is a behavioral psychologist in the employ of a fascist state. He is said to be "a manipulator and coordinator of symbol systems, an expert in all phases of interrogation, brainwashing and control" (*NL*, 21). He considers "brutality" inefficient, preferring the generalized guilt which can be induced in "free" and decent citizens (*NL*, 21). Everyone has something to hide, and all that one has to do is find what that it is. Drugs, vague threats, sexual humiliation, psychoanalytic suggestion, and other techniques can be used to reduce the citizen to a state of cringing, guilt-ridden helplessness. Carl Peterson is young, clean-cut, heterosexual, decent, ordinary, and dull, but like most people, he has memories and feelings that he would rather forget. Benway helps him to remember them and, having thereby evoked guilt and fear of exposure, is in a position to make Carl act however the occasion requires.

In *Naked Lunch*, people respond to the world mechanically rather than affectively. They are understood in terms of neurology rather than emotion, reflexes rather than pain. External stimuli rather than the subconscious dictate behavior, and the individual is a complex of conditioned reflexes. One reason the book is so shocking is that it is completely unflinching in its vision of people transformed into machines. In *Naked Lunch*, Burroughs had shifted his reportorial eye from a sociological to a psychological vision of oppression.

The final routine in *Naked Lunch* involves Hauser and O'Brien, two narcotics agents as addicted to their job and its sadistic pleasures as their victims are addicted to drugs. Hauser and O'Brien want to arrest William Lee, but he kills them first. The way to escape from people addicted to power is to destroy them. "My present assignment," says the narrator: "Find the live ones and *exterminate*" (*NL*, 205). Bartleby, in Melville's story, "preferred" not to do what was required or asked of him, but the penalty was isolation and eventually imprisonment and death. One cannot simply withdraw, Melville indicated, for the authorities (employers, courts, prisons) are everywhere. Burroughs has an answer, however, and that is to become an exterminator, to turn the game on its head and make the victimizers victims. One way to do this is to expose the way the game works, which is exactly what *Naked Lunch* does. It shows readers how men like Benway gain control and leaves the emperor without his clothes.

In a section of the novel withheld from the original edition but published in *Interzone*, the narrator says that "Drug addiction is perhaps a basic formula for pleasure and for life itself." He then tries to discover what the secret is that makes the formula work and at first decides that "the secret is that there is no secret." But reflecting on this, he decides, "I was wrong. There *is* a secret, now in the hands of ignorant and evil men."[19] He does not say what the secret is, but given Burroughs's obsession in subsequent books with language as a "virus," one might assume that the secret involves words and communication.

That idea may also be suggested by a chapter entitled "Words" and withheld from the original edition of the novel. Eventually published in *Interzone*, it shows Burroughs doing something very similar to what Kerouac did in "Old Angel Midnight." Words are strung together primarily as sounds rather than for meaning. The language is heavily scatological and obscene, and the effect is ultimately tedious and boring. It ends in a "vast Moslem muttering."[20] Words are reduced to "muttering," and their power to shock is exorcised.

The people in Interzone are divided into a number of groups which, except for one called the Factualists, are interested in seeing that everyone be like them or at least be under their control. The factualists are in effect Americans before business and bureaucracy organized life and values. "Bureaucracy is wrong as a cancer," according to *Naked Lunch*, "a turning away from the human evolutionary direction of infinite potentials and differentiation and independent spontaneous action, to the complete parasitism of a virus" (*NL*, 134).

Burroughs's values seem in some measure to have been derived from an earlier America, the West, the frontier—everything to which St. Louis was at one time considered the gateway. He is a libertarian, and, like Thoreau's *Walden* and Emerson's *Nature*, *Naked Lunch* would free the individual from convention and the State. As Burroughs told Gerard Malanga, "Well, I think the self, what you call your *self*, is like the tip of the iceberg. . . . If you could contact all your own abilities—uh, your abilities are incredible!"[21]

Although the book was published in Paris in 1959, an American edition did not appear until 1962. The following year a Boston bookseller was charged with selling obscenity, namely *Naked Lunch*, but after a widely publicized trial, the Massachusetts Supreme Court declared in July, 1966, that the book was not obscene.[22]

Burroughs has noted that his works "come in more or less trilogies,"[23] and his major fiction since *Naked Lunch* can in fact be grouped into three series of three related books each: *The Soft Machine* (1961, rev. 1966, 1968), *The Ticket That Exploded* (1962, rev. 1967, 1968), and *Nova Express* (1964) (collectively known as *The Nova Trilogy*); *The*

Wild Boys (1971), *Exterminator!* (1973), and *Port of Saints* (1975, rev. 1980); *Cities of the Red Night* (1981), *The Place of Dead Roads* (1983), and *The Western Lands* (1987). When he completed the last of these, he turned to his memoirs and a life of Christ. His published works since *Naked Lunch* also include many less ambitious works such as *Minutes to Go*, a collection of early cut-ups by him, Corso, Gysin, and Sinclair Beiles (1960), *The Yage Letters* (with Ginsberg, 1963); *The Last Words of Dutch Schultz*, a screenplay (1970); *Brion Gysin Let the Mice In*, cut-ups and other works by Burroughs, Gysin, and Ian Sommerville (1973); *White Subway*, cut-ups with essays by Alan Ansen and Paul Bowles (1973); *Cobble Stone Gardens*, a memoir with earlier pieces (1976); *The Third Mind*, cut-ups and other pieces by Burroughs and Gysin (1978); *Ah Pook Is Here and Other Texts*, works published earlier, together with the title work, "originally planned as a picture book modelled on the surviving Mayan codices,"[24] (1979); *Blade Runner*, a screenplay, though not for the Hollywood film produced under that name (1979); *Letters to Allen Ginsberg: 1953–1957* (1982); *The Burroughs File* (1984), a selection of new and previously published works, including *White Subway* and *Cobble Stone Gardens*; *The Adding Machine*, a collection of essays (1986); and *Interzone* (1989), a collection of early stories and other material. None of these works is as important to Burroughs's oeuvre and reputation as the novels, and generally even critics such as Eric Mottram, Jennie Skerl, and Robin Lydenberg, who have written book-length studies of Burroughs, mention these works, if at all, only in passing. They contain some of

Burroughs

Burroughs's most experimental works, especially cut-ups, but his most concerted efforts have always gone into the novels, and it is on them that his stature as a writer principally depends.

A few weeks after *Naked Lunch* was published, the artist Brion Gysin, who was among Burroughs's closest friends, cut up a newspaper and, rearranging the pieces, found that new alignment also created new meanings. Burroughs was intrigued with the results and began experimenting with cut-ups and then fold-ins—folding a page in such a way that one section of text overlaps another, creating new combinations of words. These techniques seemed to offer an important way of breaking the hold linguistic conventions had on civilization.

In 1939, Burroughs had been interested in hieroglyphics, which, he said, gave him a "key to the mechanism of possession" (*Q*, xx). He did not mean by "possession" what a psychologist would but rather something "closer to the medieval model"—the infestation of demonic forces that exorcism is intended to drive out (*Q*, xix). Hieroglyphics and cuneiform mark the beginnings of writing and consequently the ability to establish and preserve meaning.

Syntax and logic shape perception, but unexpected juxtapositions, as in collage, can have their own interest, their own meaning. Cut-ups disrupted syntax and the seeming inevitability nurtured by conventional discourse. They were not simply random arrangements of words. Chance obviously played a part in the process, but the writer still had to select from the welter of new arrangements the interesting groups of words and eliminate those which seemed merely aimless. "Remember that I first made selections," Burroughs said. "Out of hundreds of possible sentences that I might have used, I chose one."[25]

The French poet Edmond Jabès noted that since Burroughs considers language as "the seat of power," it is enough "to break language—to break the sentence—in order to destroy power by isolating it." But, Jabès continued, "to assault language, doesn't that also mean to destroy oneself with it?"[26] Indeed, as we have seen, Ginsberg thought that was exactly what Burroughs was doing. The cut-up was the ultimate ploy in dealing with an oppressive world, obliterating both the self and the system that had oppressed it.

The Soft Machine is organized randomly, and its seventeen chapters could be read in any order.[27] Routines omitted from *Naked Lunch* are included, but characters like Dr. Benway and Carl Peterson appear, only to vanish inexplicably a few pages later. People from Burroughs's life also emerge suddenly but similarly disappear without explanation. One narrative is suddenly suspended, and a new one begins.

Like the other volumes in the Nova trilogy, *The Soft Machine* repeatedly undermines traditional expectations of narrative and character and cannot be summarized or discussed in any conventional way. Jennie Skerl, who is among Burroughs's best critics, approaches the book thematically, arguing that its major theme is sexuality as a means of social control." She feels, for example that "the fantasy of Puerto Joselito in [the chapter entitled] 'Pretend an Interest.' . . . portrays primitive man as wholly enslaved by psychosexual control systems," while "Slotless

City [in 'Gongs of Violence'] is a futuristic fantasy of violence and chaos produced by sexual conflict."[28]

The book can also be discussed as a network of descriptions, truncated narratives, and so forth which transform the way in which sexuality is seen and understood. Indeed the book ultimately has to do more with perception than with ideas, and the perceptions which it tries to alter are the reader's. "I'm concerned with the precise manipulation of word and image . . . ," Burroughs said, "to create an alteration in the reader's consciousness."[29]

The Soft Machine is an attack on conventions of sexual behavior and is, like *Naked Lunch*, saturated with descriptions of sexual acts, primarily masturbation and sodomy, but these descriptions are always mechanical and rarely erotic. People are depersonalized, as in pornography, and sexuality is presented as a function rather than as a complex of feelings. The effect is to deprive sexuality of enchantment. This is not the sentimental homoeroticism of A. E. Housman's *A Shropshire Lad*, the idealized homosexuality of Stefan George, or the effete posturings of Oscar Wilde. These are in effect all "cons," ways of enchanting (through sentiment, worship, and humor) the object of desire, but they are at the same time systems which imprison those who use them, forms of sexual domination that entrap the aggressor together with the victim.

The book begins in the hard-boiled style used in *Junky* and *Queer*: "There is a boy sitting at the counter thin-faced kid his eyes all pupil. I see he is hooked and sick. Familiar face maybe from the pool hall where I scored for tea sometime."[30] As in the earlier books, the style involves a way of seeing things, one which is objective and which excludes sentiment and sentimentality. Other passages borrow from other literary modes, such as pornography and science fiction, which also involve direct, objective seeing. But these modes are then further drained of emotional force through cut-ups: "There is a boy sitting like your body. I see he is a hook. I drape myself over him from the pool hall. Draped myself over his cafeteria and his shorts dissolved in strata of subways . . . and all house flesh" (*SM*, 7, Burroughs's ellipsis). The erotic nature of the original material is suggested even in the cut-up, but its emotional power is dissolved, and the reader is confronted with the fact that it is only a style and words that he or she is dealing with.

Burroughs takes essentially pornographic material and neutralizes it by making it appear tedious and banal, and the novel is in this way actually very puritanical. Ginsberg said that "the cut-ups were originally designed to rehearse and repeat [Burroughs's] obsession with sexual images over and over again . . . and then re-combined and cut up and mixed in; so that finally the obsessive attachment, compulsion and preoccupation empty out and drain from the image."[31] The reader, in any case, is repeatedly left with the recognition that what is on the page is, after all, only words. Erotic imagery—or indeed emotionally charged language of any sort—thereby loses its force.

In spite of this, some of the cut-ups do not quite erode feeling, and nostalgia and sentiment are still evident: "Call through remote dawn of back yards and ash pits—plaintive ghost in the turnstile—Shadow cars and wind faces came to World's End—street light on soiled clothes dim jerky far away dawn in his eyes. Do you begin to see there is no boy there in the dark room? He was looking at something a long time ago. Changed place?—Same position—Sad image circulates through backwards time—'' (*SM*, 70).

The book's political intentions are clear in the chapter entitled ''The Mayan Caper,'' in which the narrator goes back through history to Mayan civilization and experiences directly the way Mayan priests dominated their people: ''I felt the crushing weight of evil insect control forcing my thoughts and feelings into prearranged molds, squeezing my spirit in a soft invisible vise'' (*SM*, 93). The narrator gains access to the Mayan codices and makes cut-ups from them, dissolving their syntax and hence their meaning and their power to control. All that is left is the vocabulary and the images they evoke: ''you see the priests *were* nothing but word and image, an old film rolling on and on with dead actors'' (*SM*, 97).

The narrator in ''The Mayan Caper'' is like the Factualists in *Naked Lunch*, seeing things as they are rather than as those in control intend them to be seen. The world becomes fact and action rather than abstraction and illusion of meaning. As Burroughs had learned from Korzybski, one should distrust words which do not have a clear factual reference, and *The Soft Machine* seeks to expose ways in which language controls feeling and behavior.

As Eric Mottram has argued, the object in the second volume of the Nova trilogy, *The Ticket That Exploded*, ''is freedom from mythology—what Edward Dahlberg calls freedom from living mythically.''[32] The world we perceive is determined in large measure by the language we speak, and we filter and understand experience through myth. As Burroughs argues in an afterword, "what we see is determined to a large extent by what we hear."[33] The Nova Mob want to "create as many insoluble conflicts as possible and always aggravate existing conflicts" (*TTE*, 55). Their principal battleground is language, in which conflict and contradiction are easily established. To destroy the Mob, one needs to undermine words. According to the afterword, one way to evade their tyranny is to use a tape recorder to break "old association locks" (*TTE*, 208–9). By erasing certain sections and recording over others, one "can influence and create events" (*TTE*, 207). Changing the way words are heard, one changes the world: "Get it out of your head and into the machines. Stop talking stop arguing. Let the machines talk and argue. A tape recorder is an externalized section of the human nervous system. You can find out more about the nervous system and gain more control over your reaction by using a tape recorder than you could find out sitting twenty years in the lotus posture" (*TTE*, 163).

Taking his own advice, Burroughs uses tape recordings as well as cut-ups and fold-ins to disrupt the patterns of language and expose, among other things, the violence embedded in it: "Wooden pegs in another room forgotten memory controlling the structure of his Scandinavian outhouse skin—The man flicked Ali's clothes—Prisoner pants with wriggling movement stood naked now in green mummy flesh, hanging vines and deflated skin—Death kissed him—His breath talked to the switchblade—" (*TTE*, 41).

"An initial reading of this fragmented narrative is disorienting, frustrating, almost physically unpleasant,"

Robin Lydenberg has said. "Each chapter title promises a particular focus, but it is rarely maintained; instead one stumbles repeatedly over fragments of other routines and other texts."[34] But disorientation is, of course, the way out of the fixation that language has on the mind. Fighting his enemies on their own ground, Burroughs creates greater conflicts than they do; as in *The Soft Machine*, he dissolves the expectations and certainties of semantic order, thereby leaving members of the Nova Mob mumbling nonsense.

The Nova Police, whose spokesman is Inspector J. Lee, are exterminators who root out the mob's influence. Lee and the police "do our work and go" (*TTE*, 54). They have in effect, like Burroughs, a ticket for anyone who wants to take a journey out of language, but because they aren't imposing anything of their own on the world, even the ticket explodes.

The book ends with a calligraphic work by Brion Gysin in which Arabic script and English words ("to say good silence by") dissolve into a labyrinth of curves and lines that look at first like letters but prove, on closer examination, to be pure abstract design. Words are defeated; silence reigns.

The Nova trilogy is obviously a very political, ideologically motivated work. Eric Mottram has called the third volume, *Nova Express*, "openly didactic,"[35] Certainly any one who missed the ideological intentions behind the first two volumes would not miss it here. Once again there is an extensive use of cut-ups or fold-ins to disrupt language and meaning. Passages used earlier in the trilogy are introduced again, and the same characters emerge and disappear. The Nova Mob meets its match only in the Nova Police, although, as Burroughs has said, they begin to seem "an ambivalent agency"—"like police anywhere."[36] The point is that as soon as the police take action, the Mob has succeeded in what after all is their sole objective: to create opposition.

Similarly, language creates differences and distinctions, which are essentially forms of opposition, and so in *Nova Express*, as throughout the trilogy, the only real solution is silence. That in particular is the subject of a chapter entitled "Last Words," which, as one might expect from an author who disrupts all conventional expectations, is actually the first chapter in the book. Burroughs here introduces Hassan i Sabbah, the man who wanted to "*rub out the word forever.*"[37]

Toward the end of the eleventh century, the historical Hassan i Sabbah (or, more correctly, Hasan ibn al-Sabbah) founded in Persia an Islamic sect called the Ismailis or the Nizaris, known in the West as the Assassins. An "assassin" in Arabic is a person who uses hashish, and the Ismailis, or at least the elite among them, were in effect professional murderers who used hashish preparatory to killing. Hassan i Sabbah is remembered for the dictum, frequently repeated in Burroughs's works: "Nothing is true. Everything is permitted." The first half of that dictum does not mean that there is no truth, but rather that what is true is "nothing" or nothingness. The truth in language is in effect the silence between the sounds. Hassan i Sabbah would "*rub out the word*" but not the silence which surrounds it.

Language, a virus controlled by the Nova Mob, promises a "Garden of Delights," "*love love love* in slop buckets," "Immortality Cosmic Consciousness," and so forth (in short, the sort of things flower children, at the time the novel was published, were searching for), but, Burroughs reports, "their Garden of Delights is a terminal sewer—I have been at some pains to map this area of terminal sewage in the so called pornographic sections of *Naked Lunch* and *Soft Machine*—Their Immortality Cosmic Consciousness is second-run grade-B shit" (*NE*, 13–14).

Nova Express twists through routines and cut-ups, undermining language and the Nova Mob to end finally in "*Silence*—Don't answer—That hospital melted into air—The great wind revolving turrets towers palaces—Insubstantial sound and image flakes fall—" (*NE*, 186). Having reached that point, "You are yourself—There be—" (*NE*, 186–87).

That statement is followed, however, by the words, "Well that's about the closest way I know to tell you and papers rustling across city desks . . . fresh southerly winds a long time ago" (*NE*, 361, Burroughs's ellipsis). The tone is unmistakably elegiac. Burroughs may have considered himself a Factualist, but his cut-ups could not eliminate here, as elsewhere in the trilogy, a distinct elegiac and nostalgic current—a current which became much stronger in his subsequent books. His best work from *The Wild Boys* (1971) to *The Western Lands* (1987) can be very nostalgic indeed, exploiting fantasies associated with adolescence and with memories of Burroughs's life in St. Louis.

Among Burroughs's influences in these later novels is another writer from Missouri, Mark Twain. Audrey Carsons in *The Wild Boys* is a version of Huck Finn. It is 1920, and Audrey lives on in St. Louis on Pershing Avenue (the street of middle-class homes where Burroughs lived as a boy). His friend, John Hamlin, lives on Portland Place (an actual street of grand mansions not far from Pershing). Audrey drives "a battered Moon," but Hamlin has "a magnificent Dusenberg [sic]," and one day he takes Audrey on a hair-raising drive to St. Joseph for lunch.[38] Audrey imagines the Duesenberg in a splendid explosion destroying people who would oppress him, but then the car, intact again, reaches a fairgrounds with a penny-arcade peep show where Audrey is shown extraordinary visions. He sees himself, among other things, as a landlocked Huck Finn, and Huck's raft becomes a "reconstructed houseboat firmly moored between the branches of a giant oak and secured by anchor chains to an overhead branch" (*WB*, 162). Here Audrey and "Kiki the Mexican boy who lives down by the railroad tracks" (*WB*, 163) live a bucolic fantasy as far from the propriety, rigidity, and, above all, hypocrisy of middle-class America as did Huck and Jim on the Mississippi. If one can no longer escape on a raft, there are penny arcades in the mind.

Watching visions in the arcade, Audrey is able to pass back and forth through time as in a dream. Time travel here and in other Burroughs novels (it is a major factor in structuring volumes in the second and third trilogies) is more than a device to develop the narrative; by splicing two eras together, he in effect extends the cut-up to show what is oppressive in one period and how little survives it. Just as Burroughs had earlier cut up language, here he sets out to destroy the syntax of calendars and clocks.

Several chapters and passages are specifically concerned with the visions of the penny-arcade peep show, but in effect the whole novel is a series of peep-show visions, and the narrative cuts rapidly from one incident or image to another, moving from the past (1920) to the present (1969, the year the book was written), to the future (1988). The past is represented by people like Colonel Greenfield, "one of the truly great bores of St. Louis," who believes the world on the other side of the Atlantic is "a sink of iniquity" (*WB*, 29, 122). "You may say that what happens in a foreign land is no concern of ours," he says. "But the vile tentacles of that evil are reaching into decent American homes" (*WB*, 122–23). Indeed they are, for beginning in Marrakech in 1969, bands of wild boys have fanned out to dominate the world, and American boys have hurried to join them. The wild boys are able to reproduce themselves and so no longer depend on women.

Burroughs said that book takes place in the interval described in *The Tibetan Book of the Dead* "in which the person doesn't know that he's dead and undergoes all sorts of adventures and difficulties and then is reborn or not reborn as the case may be." *The Wild Boys* then is "a picture of the period between death and rebirth,"[39] a moment potentially free of viruses like language that control the living world. "We intend to march on the police machine everywhere," writes one on his way to join the wild boys. "We intend to destroy the police machine and all its records. We intend to destroy all dogmatic verbal systems" (*WB*, 139–40).

The wild-boy gangs expand throughout the world. Rather than retreat to a raft, they eventually dominate civilization and take revenge on their oppressors. In a final series of visions that pass before Audrey's face at the penny-arcade peep show, "the roller-skate boys sweep down a hill in a shower of autumn leaves. They slice through a police patrol. Blood splatters dead leaves in air'' (*WB*, 184).

Burroughs said that, although his next major book, *Exterminator!*, was published as a novel, he thought of it as "a collection of related short pieces,"[40] and actually it is difficult to see how one could consider it otherwise. The book ranges from collections of jottings ("Cold Lost Marbles") to journalism ("The Coming of the Purple Better One") to what is at least in part autobiography (" 'Exterminator!' ") to routines. "The Lemon Kid," however, is a well-crafted story that could have been a chapter in *The Wild Boys*. Here Audrey Carsons learns how to use words to create people as real as those who passed before his eyes in the penny arcade. In a night club, a woman is doing a terrible rendition of "Ain't She Sweet." All that Audrey has to do is block out her sound and imagine that the singer is The Lemon Kid, who sings the song outrageously, then turns to the audience, which has been singing along with him, "and shoves his lemon in every bellowing mouth."[41] One can imagine the world to be whatever one wants; as in all Burroughs's novels beginning with *The Wild Boys*, people save themselves from the world by imagining another.

Port of Saints incorporates miscellaneous episodes originally written for, but not included in, *The Wild Boys*. (Burroughs's biographer Ted Morgan in fact remarked that *Port of Saints* could have been titled *The Further Adventures of the Wild Boys* or *Wild Boys Redux*.[42]) The key episode is again Audrey's magical ride in John Hamlin's Duesenberg, which this time takes place on October 23,

1925, rather than 1929 or 1920. "Adventure was a virtual impossibility in a midwestern matriarchy," Burroughs writes,[43] but John Hamlin offers the key to fantasies over which matriarchs have no control. According to a story Audrey has been writing, Hamlin died in a car accident—presumably the accident which, according to *The Wild Boys*, happened in 1920 (*PS*, 62). But here the Duesenberg is intact, and Hamlin and Audrey are off. The landscape through which they drive this time is not Missouri, however, but northern Africa: "it looked flat and dusty and there were people by the side of the road dressed in white robes" (*PS*, 63). The boys go to the fairgrounds again, populated only by adolescent boys with a few older men. Hamlin and Audrey leave the car, walk through the fair, turn a corner, and find themselves mysteriously back in St. Louis except that now Portland Place and the Hamlin house no longer seem as well kept as they should be. The lawn is full of weeds, and the sidewalk is cracked. They go to Hamlin's bedroom. At his suggestion, they have sex, and as they do, Audrey's "head [explodes] in pictures" (*PS*, 66).

The penny arcade gave Audrey his visions in *The Wild Boys*, but this time he finds them through sex. John Hamlin, roaring over the back roads of Missouri in his Duesenberg, has escaped matriarchal St. Louis. He is like Ishmael on the *Pequod*, free of women and domesticity but equally driven toward death. In one sequence, John signs on as third mate on the *Mary Celeste* (a historical ship from which all crew and passengers mysteriously disappeared), where Audrey is his cabin boy, but he is sick with tuberculosis and is called "the ice boy." The *Mary Celeste* will disappear from history, and John and Audrey will be together outside time: "I'm Audrey your chill of interstellar space," he tells John (*PS*, 126).

In another sequence, Audrey goes to John's summer house. No one is home, and he goes up the stairs: "The room is empty—no bed, no chairs, only the blue wallpaper with ship scenes and wooden pegs where we hung our clothes. No curtains at the window and one pane has a hole in it made by an air rifle. Nothing, nobody there. Standing at the window, looking down at the moss and some late forget-me-nots. Yellow hair in the morning wind standing at the window, the call of a mourning dove, frogs croaking in the creek, the church bell, a little postcard town fading into the blue lake and sky . . . " (*PS*, 145–46).

As in the cut-ups in the Nova trilogy, *Port of Saints* evokes feelings of nostalgia and loss—memories of ecstasies that have vanished leaving only empty rooms. To prevent loss, Audrey establishes his Death Academy, devoted to training students against the death virus. Students "experience death in many forms" (*PS*, 151), so that they can know how to recognize and evade it. Audrey's answer to death is to develop transcendently powerful imaginations that move through space and time at will: the Duesenberg explodes, but a split second later, John Hamlin is back at the wheel, and indeed at the end of *Port of Saints*, Audrey and John are together again, and "the Duesenberg disappears over the hills and far away . . . fading streets a distant sky . . . " (*PS*, 174).

Audrey is a writer who even at sixteen "possessed the writer's self-knowledge and self-disgust, and the God-guilt all writers feel in creation" (*PS*, 59). Writing becomes his escape from matriarchy and his revenge on it. At one point, Colonel Greenfield's wife says that Audrey is "a walking corpse." When she dies some years later, Audrey responds, "It isn't every corpse that can walk." "The mills of a writer grind slowly," the book continues, "but they grind exceedingly fine" (*PS*, 60).

In his second trilogy, Burroughs creates an ideal adolescent world as an escape from those moral rigidities and conformist pressures attacked throughout his work, but in his third trilogy he tries to find a way out through fantasy. As in *Port of Saints*, Burroughs offers the imagination as an escape from the repressions and rigidities imposed by society. By the end of the trilogy, the ultimate inadequacy of this solution is clear, however.

Cities of the Red Night weaves together three apocalyptic stories. The principal story involves the cities themselves and the violence which overwhelmed them a hundred thousand years ago. A second deals with eighteenth-century pirate boys and their attempt to create a utopia. The third, set in the present, involves the detective Clem Snide and his search for missing boys. Spanning the millenia between the cities of the red night and the present is the B-23 virus: love. As always in Burroughs's work, romantic affection is a disease; the only desirable condition is freedom, and the utopia which the pirates want to establish is a place where boys can live as they please, something perhaps like the land of the lost boys in *Peter Pan*. The book concludes with characters from all three narratives brought together in a gigantic warehouse to perform a play called "Cities of the Red Night." It appears that everything happens at the moment it is written by Audrey, who finally types out the words "The Rescue," at which moment the warehouse collapses, and everything dissolves (*CRN*, 330). The rescue or salvation occurs, as in *The Wild Boys*, in destruction and death.

In his foreword (entitled "*FORE!*"), Burroughs talks about an eighteenth-century pirate, Captain Mission, who tried to establish a colony he called Libertatia. It was to operate under libertarian principles, but its citizens were slaughtered in an unexpected attack, and the captain was himself killed a short while later. Had he and others who tried to create similar colonies succeeded, the world might have been somewhat different, Burroughs says, but as it is, "there is simply no room left for 'freedom from the tyranny of government' since city dwellers depend on it for food, power, water, transportation, protection, and welfare. Your right to live where you want, with companions of your choosing, under laws to which you agree, died in the eighteenth century with Captain Mission. Only a miracle or a disaster could restore it" (*CRN*, xv).

Audrey provides the necessary miracle through his imagination and words, but he can only *propose* solutions—he cannot make them real. There is no final escape from the world, and the narrator, presumably Burroughs himself, concludes the book by saying, "I remember a dream of my childhood. I am in a beautiful garden. As I reach out to touch the flowers they wither under my hands. A nightmare feeling of foreboding and desolation comes over me as a great mushroom-shaped cloud darkens the earth. A few may get through the gate in time. . . . I am bound to the past" (*CRN*, 332).[44]

Cities of the Red Night was intended to be a conventional novel—conventional at least in comparison to Burroughs's earlier fiction—but its three principal narratives (each written in a different style) and various subsidiary stories create a collage similar to *Naked Lunch*. Burroughs's next novel, *The Place of Dead·Roads* (1983), is structurally more clear-cut and orthodox, although time-travel provides the same narrative freedom Burroughs had in *Port of Saints*.

The hero of *The Place of Dead Roads*, Kim Carsons, is a vision of Audrey Carsons as a boy shootist—the crack shot who does what other boys can only dream of doing. He is, however, "everything a normal American boy is taught to *detest*. He is evil and slimy and *insidious*."[45] He prefers men to women and considers "romantic love . . . disgusting, rather like the cult of Southern womanhood" (*PDR*, 18). He also has a great love of guns, a passion shared by his creator.

Kim is not liked at home in St. Louis, and "as a prisoner serving a life sentence can think only of escape, [he] takes it for granted that the only purpose of his life is space travel" (*PDR*, 40). He learns space travel, and the book then tracks his adventures by jumping back and forth in time. Among other things, he establishes his own group of outlaws, the Wild Fruits, who antagonize Colonel Greenfield, and he founds the Johnson Family, a group of men whom "decent" citizens find suspicious but who can be relied on to do whatever is truly good and decent. In the end Kim is killed during a gunfight by someone (unnamed) who comes from behind and takes him by surprise.

Burroughs says that Billy the Kid walked into a dark room and, knowing someone was there, asked, "*Quién es?*" ("Who is it?"). The answer was a blast from Pat Garrett's rifle. In the end, Kim is confident that he will be able to shoot his opponent in the showdown before the opponent can shoot him, but in his confidence, he has not recognized his true enemy. Facing his opponent, he sees the man suddenly crumple, shot by someone out of Kim's range. *Quién es?* Kim is slapped on the back: he "*hates* being slapped on the back. He turns in angry protest . . . blood in his mouth . . . can't turn . . . the sky darkens and goes out" (*PDR*, 306, Burroughs's ellipses).

Audrey Carsons was able to write a book that altered the past; Kim Carsons was able to speed through time creating heroes where there had been none. *The Western Lands* attempts the ultimate triumph over time: "winter . . . is Old Age, the last test and the toughest."[46] William Seward Hall "sets out to write his way out of death" (*WL*, 3). As in the earlier books in the trilogy, the key to the way out is fantasy, but fantasy, Hall finds, cannot transform death or explain it: it can not answer the final question: *Quién es?* With imagination and words, Hall wants to find the ultimate paradise, the Western Lands, but more than writing is required to reach that destination. There is no apocalypse at the end of the novel, no *Pequod* trailing the great whale to the bottom of the sea, but simply William Seward Hall, alone with memories. He can't "write anymore because he [has] reached the end of words, the end of what can be done with words" (*WL*, 258). *The Western Lands* is Burroughs's *Pilgrim's Progress* without a celestial city at the end of the road.

Burroughs

According to *The Western Lands*, Kim was killed by Joe the Dead, a revenant who is able to reshape nature to his own liking. Joe is thoroughly unscrupulous and amoral. He practices "a purity of function that [can] be maintained only by the pressure of deadly purpose" (*WL*, 29). "Cause and effect" is, he believes, a "monumental fraud," and he would see it "replaced by the more pregnant concept of synchronicity" (*WL*, 30).

The trilogy suggests much the same thing: traditional chains of cause and effect are what allow such people as Colonel Greenfield to keep their power, while synchonicity permits time travel, the ability to escape from the rigidities of cause and effect. Dreams, Burroughs writes, "are a biologic necessity and your lifeline to space, that is, to the state of a God"—one way of transcending cause and effect, time and space (*WL*, 181). But "the state of a God" is forbidden by society, and as Burroughs points out the Ismailis were persecuted because they took on "the prerogatives of the Creator—and in a very literal sense, for his aim was the creation of new beings" (*WL*, 198). That has always been the messianic object of Burroughs's work as well—the transfiguration of his readers, thereby creating free individuals in a world of conformists. In the world of Islam, one was not to be a God but a "mullah"—a theologian or an interpreter of the law rather than a creator. "Leadership," the book notes, "is passed along by direct contact with the Imam, in the course of which the subject becomes the Imam" (*WL*, 198). A civilization preserves itself in short through duplication and perfect conformity.

But the divinity of dreams and fantasies still does not reveal the answer to the question *Quién es*? In the end, the dreamer is always brought back to the fact that he or she is not omnipotent. At the end of the book the narrator recalls that "hectic, portentous time in Paris, in 1959" when he was living in the "Beat Hotel" and experimenting in magic. But nearly thirty years have passed and "here I am in Kansas with my cats, like the honorary agent for a planet that went out light-years ago" (*WL*, 252).

He remembers, "There were moments of catastrophic defeat, and moments of triumph. The pure killing purpose. You find out what it means to lose. Abject fear and ignominy. Still fighting, without the means to fight. Deserted. Cut off. . . . Every man for himself—if he's got a self left. Not many do" (*WL*, 253).

"The pure killing purpose" is, like dreams, not enough, however. Joe the Dead has absolute determination, but he does not make it to the Western Lands. Neither does the narrator. Imagination and desire are not adequate in themselves.

At the end, the narrator asks, "How long does it take a man to learn that he does not, cannot want what he 'wants'?" (*WL*, 257). Korzybski's distinction between the imagined and the real returns to undercut fantasy as an escape. One does not have, and therefore literally cannot know, what one "wants." It is only another illusion. In the end, there is only the world as given at the moment of writing.

In this recognition, *The Western Lands* is as much a powerful admission of failure as Kerouac's *Big Sur*; both books attest to the fact that imagination and writing are not therapy, and although there are moments of grace, writing always returns the writer where he began, without illusions.

There is no paradise that will last, at least none the writer will find in words. In its disciplined integrity, *The Western Lands* is as crucial to Burroughs's work as *Big Sur* is to Kerouac's.

Notes

1. Quoted in Ted Morgan, *Literary Outlaw: The Life and Times of William S. Burroughs* (New York: Henry Holt, 1988) 52.

2. William S. Burroughs, "Who Did What Where and When?" *The Adding Machine* (New York: Seaver, 1986) 159.

3. William S. Burroughs, *Cities of the Red Night* (New York: Holt, Rinhart and Winston, 1981) 332. Subsequent references are given parenthetically in the text.

4. William S. Burroughs, "The Fall of Art," *The Adding Machine* (New York: Seaver, 1986) 61.

5. Burroughs's relation to hipster culture is discussed in Jennie Skerl, *William S. Burroughs* (Boston: Twayne, 1985) 7 and passim.

6. Herbert S. Huncke, "From *Guilty of Everything*," *Kerouac and the Beats*, ed. Arthur and Kit Knight (New York: Paragon, 1988) 72.

7. William S. Burroughs, *Naked Lunch* (New York: Grove, 1962) vii. The ellipsis is Burroughs's. Subsequent references are given parenthetically in the text.

8. William S. Burroughs, "Lee's Journal," *Interzone* (New York: Viking Penguin, 1989) 71. Subsequent references are given parenthetically in the text.

9. Morgan, *Literary Outlaw*, 214.

10. William S. Burroughs, *Junky* (New York: Penguin, 1977) 1. Subsequent references are given parenthetically in the text.

11. William S. Burroughs, *Queer* (New York: Viking Penguin, 1985) 39. Subsequently referrred to in parentheses in the text.

12. William S. Burroughs and Allen Ginsberg, *The Yage Letters* (San Francisco: City Lights, 1963) 44. Subsequent references are given parenthetically in the text.

13. The working title for *Naked Lunch* was "Interzone"; the published title was suggested by Kerouac and had been used in Ginsberg's poem "On

Burroughs' Work," written in 1954. The description of Interzone from *The Yage Letters* reappears in *Naked Lunch*, pp. 106–7. Burroughs himself has said that Interzone was based on Tangiers. See William S. Burroughs, *Letters to Allen Ginsberg: 1953–1957* (New York: Full Court, 1982) 77.

14. William S. Burroughs and Kells Elvins, "Twilight's Last Gleaming," *Interzone* (New York: Viking Penguin, 1989) 4.

15. William S. Burroughs, *Letters to Allen Ginsberg: 1953–1957* (New York: Full Court, 1982), 78, 37. Subsequent references are given parenthetically in the text.

16. William S. Burroughs, "Ginsberg Notes," *Interzone* (New York: Viking Penguin, 1989) 129–30.

17. Quoted in Lionel Trilling, *Sincerity and Authenticity* (Cambridge: Harvard University Press, 1972) 119.

18. The Olympia Press edition, published in 1959, was called *The Naked Lunch*. The title became *Naked Lunch* for the American edition.

19. William S. Burroughs, "The Conspiracy," *Interzone* (New York: Viking Penguin, 1989) 110–11.

20. William S. Burroughs, "Word," *Interzone* (New York: Viking Penguin, 1989) 194.

21. Gerard Malanga, "William Burroughs and Gerard Malanga Talk," *The Beat Vision*, ed. Arthur and Kit Knight (New York: Paragon, 1987) 213.

22. Michael B. Goodman, *Contemporary Literary Censorship: The Case History of Burroughs' Naked Lunch* (Metuchen, NJ, and London: Scarecrow, 1981) traces the legal problems associated with the book.

23. George Wedge and Steven Lowe, "An Interview with William S. Burroughs," *Cottonwood* 41 (Fall 1988): 45.

24. William S. Burroughs, *Ah Pook Is Here and Other Texts* (London: Calder, 1979) 11.

25. Conrad Knickerbocker, "William Burroughs: An Interview," *Paris Review* 9 (Fall 1965): 30.

26. Edmond Jabès, *From the Desert to the Book: Dialogues with Marcel Cohen*, trans. Pierre Joris (Barrytown, NY: Station Hill, 1990) 97.

27. Burroughs in fact continued to work on both *The Soft Machine* and *The Ticket That Exploded* after their original French publications in France, and they were revised extensively before publication in the U.S. and Great Britain. As there was no model that Burroughs could follow, he could only shuffle and alter the contents while intuitively looking for some satisfactory order.

28. Skerl, *William S. Burroughs*, 52, 54, 55.

29. Knickerbocker, "William Burroughs," 49.

30. William S. Burroughs, *The Soft Machine* (New York: Grove, 1966) 9–10. Subsequent references are given parenthetically in the text.

31. Allen Young, "Allen Ginsberg," *Gay Sunshine Interviews*, Vol. I, ed. Winston Leyland (San Francisco: Gay Sunshine, 1978) 124.

32. Eric Mottram, *William Burroughs: The Algebra of Need* (London: Boyars, 1977) 78.

33. William S. Burroughs, *The Ticket That Exploded* (New York: Grove, 1967) 205–6. Subsequent references are given parenthetically in the text.

34. Robin Lydenberg, *Word Cultures: Radical Theory and Practice in William S. Burroughs' Fiction* (Urbana and Chicago: University of Illinois Press, 1987) 72.

35. Mottram, *William Burroughs*, 102.

36. Knickerbocker, "William Burroughs," 30.

37. William S. Burroughs, *Nova Express* (New York: Grove, 1964) 12. Subsequent references are given parenthetically in the text.

38. William S. Burroughs, *The Wild Boys* (New York: Grove, 1971) 33. Subsequent references are given parenthetically in the text.

39. Jennie Skerl, "An Interview with William S. Burroughs," *Modern Language Studies* 12.3 (Summer 1982): 6.

40. Skerl, "William S. Burroughs," 5.

41. William S. Burroughs, *Exterminator!* (New York: Viking/Seaver, 1973) 12. Subsequent references are given parenthetically in the text.

42. Morgan, *Literary Outlaw*, 467.

43. William S. Burroughs, *Port of Saints* (Berkeley, CA: Blue Wind, 1980) 60. Subsequent references are given parenthetically in the text.

44. This is an extremely effective way to end the book, but it appears from comments made by James Grauerholz, Burroughs's assistant, that this passage was originally located earlier in the text. Brion Gysin suggested that it be placed at the end. Nicholas Zurbrugg, "Burroughs, Grauerholz, and *Cities of the Red Night*: An Interview with James Grauerholz," *Review of Contemporary Fiction* 4.1 (1984) 23.

45. William S. Burroughs, *The Place of Dead Roads* (New York: Holt, Rinehart and Winston, 1983) 16. Subsequent references are given parenthetically in the text.

46. William S. Burroughs, *The Western Lands* (New York, Viking Penguin, 1987) 12. Subsequent references are given parenthetically in the text.

CHAPTER SIX

After the Deluge

The subject matter is really the operation of the mind.

—Allen Ginsberg,
in an interview with William Packard
collected in *The Poet's Craft*

A second generation of beat writers developed soon after "Howl" and *On the Road* were published. Diane di Prima read "Howl" when it first appeared and immediately recognized "that this Allen Ginsberg, whoever he was, had broken ground for all of us."[1] She soon met, and became friends with, Corso, Ginsberg, and Kerouac, and together with LeRoi Jones (Amiri Baraka), she edited *The Floating Bear*, one of the major publications for beat writing in the 1960s.

Di Prima, whose first book, *This Kind of Bird Flies Backward*, was published in 1958, deserves more attention than she has received. She mastered very early a colloquial style which is derived perhaps from William Carlos Williams but which is distinctly her own. At its best, as in "Poem in Praise of My Husband (Taos)," her work has considerable range, rapidly modulating with apparent ease among such extremes as determination, generosity, and self-awareness: "I suppose it hasn't been easy living with me either, / with my piques, and ups and downs, and need for privacy."[2]

Di Prima is representative of a loose network of young bohemian writers for whom the term "beat" provided a collective identity in the late 1950s, but these writers— Baraka is another good example—were not disciples or stu-

After the Deluge

dents of the original Beats. They began writing before the
Beats became known. However, "Howl," *On the Road,*
Gasoline, and *Naked Lunch,* soon after their publication,
reached and influenced many younger writers. The playwright Sam Shepard, for example, left home in southern
California largely because of "the whole beat generation"
and eventually settled in New York, where he was first
known as the drummer for the Holy Modal Rounders, and
then became famous as a playwright. "From time to time,"
he said, "I've practiced Jack Kerouac's discovery of jazz-
sketching with words. Following the exact same principles
as a musician does when he's jamming." Originally Shepard wrote very quickly, once in fact finishing a play in a
single day, and, like Kerouac, he did not revise. Michael
Smith, a *Village Voice* theater critic, saw an early Shepard
play and "was simply astonished by it because it was like
he was a bop playwright. It was like that spontaneous prosody of Ginsberg, Kerouac—what they were to poetry and
the novel."[3]

Like Kerouac, Shepard is concerned with an earlier
America, but there is considerable difference between, for
example, Kerouac's romantic vision of the West and the
"True West" Shepard portrays in his play of that title. In
that work, the brothers Austin and Lee have a symbiotic relationship vaguely reminiscent of Kerouac and Cassady's.
(Like Kerouac, Austin is an amanuensis for the other man,
who is the more daring and adventurous of the two.) But
there is none of Kerouac's tenderness in *True West,* and the
play celebrates a male stoicism and independence quite unlike anything in *On the Road* and *Visions of Cody.* Both of
these novels end in solitude, but they involve a search for

some kind of transcendent community. The only kinds of community possible in *True West* are a corrupt, money-making world and the frigid domesticity represented by "Mom," who fittingly goes to Alaska for her vacation. Men live in the desert where, like Austin and Lee at the end of the play, they are implacable enemies.

A very different sort of writer influenced by Kerouac is Tom Robbins. (There is in fact a person named Kerouac in *Even Cowgirls Get the Blues.*) The novelist who perhaps best represents the attitudes and ideals of the counterculture of the 1960s, Robbins took Kerouac's celebration of freedom and bleached it of anxiety and fear. In books such as *Another Roadside Attraction,* there is an engaging sweetness and faith that everything will work out in the end. In Kerouac's work, paradise is, with few exceptions, always in the past; in *Another Roadside Attraction,* it can exist anytime there is a good supply of marijuana or magic mushrooms. The novelists Ken Kesey and Jim Dodge also reflect Kerouac's influence, but only in terms of literary content, not style. Kerouac's aesthetics in fact have had much wider influence on poets than on fiction writers.

The Poetry Project, established in New York at St. Mark's Church in 1966, has been one of the principal channels through which beat aesthetics have been passed to younger writers. Among those associated with the project is Clark Coolidge, for whom "the challenge of [Kerouac's] art remains immense": "all I need do is read a few pages to regain sheer belief in the unstoppable endless volleying Everything Work."[4] Coolidge is also a musician, and much of his work is structured, like Kerouac's, in a manner derived from jazz: open-ended, spontaneous, improvised. Ker-

ouac's influence can be felt also in the poetry of Alice Notley, Bernadette Mayer, Bob Holman, Ed Sanders, and many
other innovative poets associated with the Poetry Project.
Among them is Anne Waldman, who directed the project
from 1968 to 1978. Waldman is known primarily as a performance poet, who took Ginsberg's poetics and, in such
works as "Fast Speaking Woman" and "Makeup on
Empty Space," created poems which are equally powerful
as theater.

In 1974, Waldman, together with Ginsberg, founded
the Jack Kerouac School of Disembodied Poetics at Naropa
Institute, Boulder, Colorado. In recent years, the Kerouac
School has been at least as important as St. Mark's in con-
tinuing the beat tradition. Its instructors, in addition to
Waldman and Ginsberg, have included Burroughs, Corso,
di Prima, Notley, Coolidge, and many others associated
with the Beats.[5]

Kerouac, Ginsberg, and Corso (although not Burroughs) tried to develop a poetics of voice—the literal presence of the poet in his words. So, too, did many other
writers—Charles Olson, Robert Creeley, and Michael Mc-
Clure, among them—who were anthologized in Donald Allen's *The New American Poetry* (1960). Not every poet in
that anthology was concerned with developing a poetics of
voice (Jack Spicer, for example, rejected it even as a desirable possibility), but most were, and the book had great effect in altering popular perceptions about what a poem
should be and do. When various language poets attacked
poetics of voice in the 1970s and 1980s, they simultaneously, by implication, attacked the Beats.

Understanding the Beats

In 1971, the poet Robert Grenier generated much debate when he announced in a manifesto against voice-based poetics, "I HATE SPEECH," and insisted that he wanted to avoid "the restrictions imposed by speech patterns/conventions." In their place, he looked for poetry as "writing." But Grenier, unlike some language poets, was not asking for a poetry that exemplified positions taken directly from linguistics and/or Marxist theory. As an expressionist himself, he argued for "the word way back in the head that is the thought or feeling forming out the 'vast' silence/noise of consciousness experiencing world *all the time,* as waking/dreaming, words occurring and *these are the words of the poems.*"[6] As Grenier pointed out, speech has its own conventions and so by implication can limit the range of possible expression as much as any poetic custom.

Kerouac, Ginsberg, and Corso did not restrict themselves to the conventions of American speech—a fact which should be clear to anyone who listens carefully, for example, to the way "Howl" is structured or to "The Geometric Poem" or to the opening paragraph of *Tristessa.* The first draws on rhetorical patterns in Christopher Smart and the Bible, the second integrates words and drawings, and the last is much closer to the process of thought than to speech. Corso incorporated inversions and archaic diction into his poetry, Kerouac explored patterns of pure sound, and Ginsberg transformed journal entries into poems. But although all three drew on many different resources for their language, they also used rhythms and diction which are more conventionally found in spoken, rather than written, English.

After the Deluge

All three, furthermore, assumed that there is a "subject" or speaker behind the words, who is revealed in them. As French literary theory began to influence American critics and poets, the assumption that the poet might somehow be personally present in the language of the poem was soon under attack. According to Roland Barthes, the belief that an author could personally be in charge of, and present in, a text was simply a bourgeois myth. The idea of the autonomous author has political implications, as George Hartley suggested: "Poetry . . . , which functions according to the notion of the poet/speaker as an independent subject who, having 'found his voice,' presents a situation seen from a single point of view, fosters the key ideological concept of bourgeois society: the self-sufficient, self-determined individual free to participate in the marketplace."[7]

In fact Burroughs had himself undermined the poetics of voice in his cut-ups and fold-ins, but he still insisted on himself as the author: he, after all, had chosen a given sentence from hundreds of possibilities. Furthermore, like the other Beats, he continued to see literature as a means through which both reader and author could be transfigured—as a means, that is, to a further consciousness. The writer was, therefore, in some ways a mage or alchemist of language. That would obviously not be a tenable position for many language poets, particularly those who saw language as strictly a social construction. From that perspective, words and understanding are purely sociopolitical phenomena, and the individual has no reality outside their context. An extreme instance of this position is the claim made by the Marxist critic V. N. Voloshinov earlier in the century that *"Outside objectification, outside embodiment in some particular material* (the material of gesture, inner words, outcry), *consciousness is a fiction."*[8] Correspondingly, all expression is utterly social and historical—not, that is, merely open to historical interpretation. The Emersonian promise of transcendence through language to an understanding beyond language—an argument developed in his essay "The Poet"—becomes in this context a fool's dream. And perhaps it is, but each individual must judge such a highly subjective matter for him- or herself. It can be argued that the theorist or poet who adopts a position like Volosinov's demeans possibilities for literature. What room is there in a view like his for Kerouac's desire, expressed in *On the Road*, to take "the complete step across time into timeless shadows"? (*OR*, 173).

The ideal for all the beat writers was to remove or transfigure the individual beyond the control of an oppressive, conformist society—which any society has the potential to be. Their concern was ultimately with matters of spiritual and personal freedom. "Howl" and "Elegiac Feelings American" show that this transfiguration has strong political implications, but the Beats continued to resist any politics that hardened into a system or form of social control, anything that would enforce conformity. Embedded in all major beat writings is the hipster's skepticism and refusal to let the writer's vision be dictated by tradition or convention.

At the same time, the Beats returned repeatedly to a recognition or fear that escape, or at least permanent escape, might not be ultimately or fully possible. Kerouac's acceptance of suffering as essential to life, Ginsberg's

After the Deluge

adoption of Williams's poetics, Corso's close reading of Randall Jarrell, and Burroughs's work with Korzybski's linguistics involve recognitions that there are boundaries the writer cannot cross or manipulate. To some degree, all beat poetry and fiction is the prisoner of personal and social conditions the writer can neither transform nor transcend.

Nonetheless, writing was for the Beats a means through which the self might be redeemed, or at the very least a place where its redemption might be recorded. When the Beats began to write, the old political solutions proposed by radical writers in the 1930s seemed ineffectual and weak beside the monolithic power of a culture which condemned difference as deviance. It was not enough to propose yet another strictly ideological solution. What was needed was a literature through which the individual could flourish beyond all factionalism, all ideologies.

That may or may not be possible, but it is a powerful reason to write, and the literature which the Beats created moves with a conviction and certainty they might never have found had they listened to their critics. At the very least, the Beats constitute an essential link in that specifically American literary tradition, traceable to Emerson and Thoreau, which insists that the individual is superior to any consensus and that poetry and fiction, in so far as they testify to this, constitute a sacred task.

Notes

1. Diane di Prima, *Memoirs of a Beatnik* (San Francisco: Last Gasp, 1988) 127.

2. Diane di Prima, *Pieces of a Song: Selected Poems* (San Francisco: City Lights, 1990).

3. Kenneth Cubb and the editors of *Theatre Quarterly*, "Metaphors, Mad Dogs and Old Time Cowboys: Interview with Sam Shepard," *American Dreams: The Imagination of Sam Shepard*, ed. Bonnie Marranca (New York: Performing Arts Journal Publications, 1981) 189; Sam Shepard, "Language, Visualization and the Inner Library," *American Dreams: The Imagination of Sam Shepard*, 217; Michael Smith quoted in Ellen Oumano, *Sam Shepard: The Life and Work of an American Dreamer* (New York: St. Martin's, 1986) 34.

4. Clark Coolidge, "A First Reading of *On the Road* and Later," *Talisman* 3 (Fall 1989): 101–2.

5. Burroughs's work has been important not only to writers, particularly poets interested in his dissection of language, but also to rock groups and performance artists. Patti Smith and Laurie Anderson are among his admirers, and his voice can be heard in "Sharkey's Night" in Anderson's *Mister Heartbreak* (1984). The term "heavy metal" is borrowed from *The Soft Machine*, the title of which became the name of a British rock group. The group Steely Dan named themselves after a sexual device in *Naked Lunch*.

6. Robert Grenier, "On Speech," in *In the American Tree*, ed. Ron Silliman (Orono, ME: National Poetry Foundation, 1986) 496. The essay originally appeared in *This* 1 (1971).

7. George Hartley, *Textual Politics and the Language Poets* (Bloomington and Indianapolis: Indiana University Press, 1989) 37.

8. V. N. Volosinov, *Marxism and the Philosophy of Language*, trans. Ladislav Matejka and I. R. Titunik (Cambridge: Harvard University Press, 1986) 90.

SELECT BIBLIOGRAPHY

General Works
Books

Bartlett, Lee, ed. *The Beats: Essays in Criticism.* Jefferson, NC: McFarland, 1981. A collection of major critical essays, all but one reprinted.

Charters, Ann, ed. *The Beats: Literary Bohemians in Postwar America,* 2 volumes. Detroit: Gale, 1983. Good introductions to beat writers and others associated with them.

Cook, Bruce, *The Beat Generation.* New York: Scribners, 1971. A popular study drawing on informative interviews.

Holmes, John Clellon. *Passionate Opinions: The Cultural Essays.* Fayetteville, AK: University of Arkansas Press, 1988; *Representative Men: The Biographical Essays.* Fayetteville, AK: University of Arkansas Press, 1988. These volumes collect Holmes's essays on the Beat Generation.

Horemans, Rudi, ed. *Beat Indeed!* Antwerp: EXA, 1985. Miscellaneous collection of reviews and commentary, mostly about Kerouac, and original work by writers influenced by the Beats.

Knight, Arthur and Kit, eds. *The Beat Vision.* New York: Paragon, 1987; *Kerouac and the Beats: A Primary Sourcebook.* New York: Paragon, 1988. Interviews and essays originally published in the journal *the unspeakable visions of the individual.* Invaluable resources for background data.

Lauridsen, Inger Thorup, and Per Dalgard. *The Beat Generation and the Russian New Wave.* Ann Arbor: Ardis, 1990. Interviews with contemporary Russian poets and with Ginsberg, McClure, Snyder, and Ferlinghetti.

Lipton, Lawrence. *The Holy Barbarians.* New York: Messner, 1959. An important early study of the Beats as a sociological phenomenon, by a close associate of Kenneth Rexroth.

McClure, Michael. *Scratching the Beat Surface.* San Francisco: North Point, 1982. An introduction to expressionist and Beat poetics; includes the best essay on Kerouac's poetry yet published.

Parkinson, Thomas, ed. *A Casebook on the Beat*. New York: Crowell, 1961. Early anthology of beat works as well as early reviews and critical essays.

Saroyan, Aram. *Genesis Angels: The Saga of Lew Welch and the Beat Generation*. New York: Morrow, 1979. Primarily concerns Welch but provides a general history of the beat movement.

Stephenson, Gregory. *The Daybreak Boys: Essays on the Literature of the Beat Generation*. Carbondale and Edwardsville: Southern Illinois University Press, 1990. Collects essays by one of the Beats' foremost critics. Strong essays on Kerouac, Ginsberg, Burroughs, Corso, Holmes, Cassady, and others.

Tytell, John. *Naked Angels: The Lives and Literature of the Beat Generation*. New York: McGraw-Hill, 1976. In-depth critical and biographical study of Burroughs, Ginsberg, and Kerouac by one of the first academic critics to recognize their serious literary intentions.

Weinberg, Jeffrey H. *Writers Outside the Margin*. Sudbury, MA: Water Row, 1986. Miscellaneous collection of commentary and observations on the Beats as well as original work by writers influenced by them.

Articles

George, Paul S. "Beat Politics: New Left and Hippie Beginnings in the Postwar Counterculture," *Cultural Politics: Radical Movements in Modern History,* ed. Jerold M. Starr. New York: Praeger, 1985. Influence primarily of Kerouac and Ginsberg on the counterculture.

O'Neil, Paul. "The Only Rebellion Around," *Life* 47 (30 November 1959): 115–30. The article which perhaps more than any other was responsible for transforming the Beats into celebrities.

Select Bibliography

Podhoretz, Norman. "The Know-Nothing Bohemians," *On the Road: Text and Criticism*, ed. Scott Donaldson. New York: Viking, 1979: 346–52. The best-known of many attacks on the Beats by critics from the literary establishment.

Stimpson, Catharine R. "The Beat Generation and the Trials of Homosexual Liberation," *Salmagundi* 58/59 (Fall/Winter 1982–83): 373–92. Homosexuality within beat culture and in its literature.

Trilling, Diana. "The Other Night at Columbia: A Report from the Academy," *Partisan Review* 26.2 (Spring 1959): 214–30. A patronizing view of the Beats by an establishment critic.

Works by William S. Burroughs

Books

Junkie [published under the pseudonym William Lee]. New York: Ace, 1953; London: Digit Books, 1957. As *Junky* [unexpurgated edition], New York: Penguin, 1977.

The Naked Lunch. Paris: Olympia Press, 1959. As *Naked Lunch,* New York: Grove, 1962; London: Calder/Olympia, 1964.

Minutes to Go, with Sinclair Beiles, Gregory Corso, and Brion Gysin. Paris: Two Cities, 1960; San Francisco: Beach, 1964.

The Exterminator, with Brion Gysin. San Francisco: Auerhahn, 1960.

The Soft Machine. Paris: Olympia, 1961; revised, New York: Grove, 1966; revised again, London: Calder and Boyers, 1968.

The Ticket That Exploded. Paris: Olympia, 1962; revised, New York: Grove, 1967; revised again, London: Calder and Boyers, 1968.

Dead Fingers Talk. London: Calder/Olympia, 1963.

The Yage Letters, with Allen Ginsberg. San Francisco: City Lights, 1963.

Nova Express. New York: Grove, 1964; London: Jonathan Cape, 1966.

The Last Words of Dutch Schultz. London: Cape Goliard, 1970; New York: Viking/Seaver, 1975.

The Wild Boys. New York: Grove, 1971; London: Calder and Boyers, 1972.

Brion Gysin Let the Mice In. West Glover, VT: Something Else, 1973.

White Subway. London: Aloes, 1973.

Exterminator! New York: Viking/Seaver, 1973; London: Calder and Boyers, 1975.

Port of Saints. London: Covent Garden, 1975; revised, Berkeley, CA: Blue Wind, 1980.

Cobblestone Gardens. Cherry Valley, NY: Cherry Valley, 1976.

Ah Pook Is Here and Other Texts. London: Calder, 1979; New York: Riverrun, 1982.

The Third Mind, with Brion Gysin. New York: Viking, 1978; London, Calder, 1979.

Blade Runner. Berkeley, CA: Blue Wind, 1979.

Cities of the Red Night. New York: Holt, Rinehart and Winston, 1981; London: Calder, 1981.

Letters to Allen Ginsberg: 1953–1957. New York: Full Court, 1982.

The Place of Dead Roads. New York: Holt, Rinehart and Winston, 1983; London: Calder, 1983.

The Burroughs File. San Francisco: City Lights, 1984.

Queer. New York: Viking Penguin, 1985: London: Pan Picador, 1986.

The Adding Machine. New York: Seaver, 1986.

The Western Lands. New York: Viking Penquin, 1987; London: Picador, 1988.

Interzone. New York: Viking Penguin, 1989.

Interviews

Bockris, Victor. *With William Burroughs: A Report from the Bunker*. New York: Seaver, 1981.

Select Bibliography

Corso, Gregory, and Allen Ginsberg. "Interview with William Burroughs," *Journal for the Protection of All Beings* 1 (1961): 79–83.

Knickerbocker, Conrad, "William Burroughs: An Interview," *Paris Review* 9 (Fall 1965): 12–49.

Masterson, Graham, and Andrew Rossabi. "William Burroughs," *Penthouse* 3 (March 1972): 44–52, 122.

Odier, Daniel. *The Job: Interviews with William S. Burroughs.* New York: Grove, 1974.

Palmer, Robert. "William Burroughs," *Rolling Stone* 108 (11 May 1972): 48–53.

Rivers, J. E. "An Interview with William S. Burroughs," *Resources for American Literary Study* 10.2 (Autumn 1980): 154–66.

Skerl, Jennie. "An Interview with William S. Burroughs," *Modern Language Studies* 12.3 (Summer 1982): 3–17.

Von Ziegesar, Peter. "Mapping the Cosmic Currents: An Interview with William Burroughs," *New Letters: A Magazine of Fine Writing* 53.1 (Fall 1986): 57–71.

Wedge, George, and Steven Lowe. "An Interview with William S. Burroughs," *Cottonwood* 41 (1988): 42–50.

(See also *The Review of Contemporary Fiction*, listed below.)

Works about Burroughs

Bibliographies

Goodman, Michael, B., with Lemuel B. Coley. *William S. Burroughs: A Reference Guide.* New York: Garland, 1990.

Maynard, Joe, and Barry Miles. *William S. Burroughs: A Bibliography, 1953–73.* Charlottesville: University Press of Virginia, 1978.

Miles Associates. *A Descriptive Catalogue of the William S. Burroughs Archive.* Ollon, Switzerland, and London: Covent

Garden and Am Here, 1973. Catalogue for the Burroughs Archive in Lichtenstein.

Biography

Morgan, Ted. *Literary Outlaw: The Life and Times of William S. Burroughs.* New York: Henry Holt, 1988. A popular work, heavily detailed with essential background information.

Books

Goodman, Michael B. *Contemporary Literary Censorship: The Case History of Burroughs' Naked Lunch.* Metuchen, NJ, and London: Scarecrow, 1981. Legal problems arising from publication of the novel.

Lydenberg, Robin. *Word Cultures: Radical Theory and Practice in William S. Burroughs' Fiction.* Urbana and Chicago: University of Illinois Press, 1987. Major work examining Burroughs's fiction in light of poststructuralist critical theory.

Mottram, Eric. *William Burroughs: The Algebra of Need.* London: Boyars, 1977. Major study of Burroughs as a modernist, his theories of language and addiction, social criticisms, and so forth.

Skerl, Jennie. *William S. Burroughs.* Boston: Twayne, 1985. Best introduction to Burroughs's work; emphasizes social context and thematic concerns.

Skerl, Jennie, and Robin Lydenberg, eds. *William S. Burroughs: At the Front: Critical Reception, 1959–1989.* Carbondale and Edwardsville: Southern Illinois University Press, 1991. Superb collection of essays on and reviews of Burroughs's work together with a brief statement by Burroughs summarizing his career and his objectives.

Special Journal Issue

The Review of Contemporary Fiction 4.1 (1984). Includes, among other pieces, Philippe Mikriammos, "The Last European Interview''; Nicholas Zurbrugg, ''Burroughs, Grauerholz, and *Cities of the Red Night*: An Interview with James Grauerholz'' (interview with Burroughs's assistant); Michael Leddy, '' 'Departed Have Left No Address': Revelation/Concealment Presence/Absence in *Naked Lunch*'' (Burroughs's efforts to erase authorial presence); Barbara L. Estrin, ''The Revelatory Connection: Inspired Poetry and *Naked Lunch*'' (the novel compared to biblical and other inspired works); Steven Shaviro, ''Burroughs' Theater of Illusion: *Cities of the Red Night*'' (Burroughs's vision as dynamic, a world of relentless destruction and creation); Nicholas Zurbrugg, ''Burroughs, Barthes, and the Limits of Intertexuality'' (Burroughs in terms of contemporary literary theory); Allan Johnson, ''The Burroughs Biopathy: William S. Burroughs' *Junky* and *Naked Lunch* and Reichian Theory'' (psychological implications of narrative points of view); Jennie Skerl, ''Freedom Through Fantasy in the Recent Novels of William S. Burroughs'' (this theme as seen in novels from *The Wild Boys* to *Cities of the Red Night*).

Sections of Books

McCarthy, Mary. ''Burroughs' *Naked Lunch*,''*The Writing on the Wall and Other Essays*. New York: Harcourt, 1970: 42–53. A key essay, one of first to assert Burroughs's achievement. Examines *Naked Lunch* as satire and humor.

Nelson, Cary. ''The End of the Body: Radical Space in Burroughs,'' *The Incarnate Word: Literature and Verbal Space*. Urbana: University of Illinois Press, 1973; 208–29. Develops the idea that Burroughs unmasks illusions embedded in language.

Porush, David. ''Cybernetics and Techno-Paranoia: Kurt Vonnegut, Jr., and William Burroughs,'' *The Soft Machine: Cybernetic Fiction*. New York: Methuen, 1985; 85–111. Examines Burroughs's attempts to escape systems and control through his fiction.

Seltzer, Alvin. "Confusion Hath Fuck His Masterpiece,"*Chaos in the Novel: The Novel in Chaos.* New York: Schocken, 1974: 330–74. Burroughs's radical aesthetics, his cut-ups, and so forth. Argues that the trilogy is less successful than *Naked Lunch,* which achieves power and coherence.

Solotaroff, Theodore. "The Algebra of Need," *The Red Hot Vacuum.* New York: Atheneum, 1970: 247–53. Important early study of Burroughs's argument that drug addiction is a paradigm of many kinds of human behavior.

Tanner, Tony. "Rub Out the Word," *City of Words.* New York: Harper and Row, 1971: 109–40. Sees Burroughs's fiction as an attempt to break down social conditioning, restoring the self to a sense of things as they are.

Articles

Bliss, Michael. "The Orchestration of Chaos: Verbal Technique in William Burroughs' *Naked Lunch,*" *enclitic* 1.1 (1977): 59–69. Stylistic devices shaping the novel; language as a form of addiction that Burroughs turns to his own ends.

Cordesse, Gérard. "The Science-fiction of William Burroughs," *Caliban* 12 (1975); 33–43. Shows how works from *Naked Lunch* to *The Wild Boys* borrow conventions ("tools") from science fiction.

Glover, David. "Utopia and Fantasy in the Late 1960s: Burroughs, Moorcock, Tolkien," *Popular Fiction and Social Change,* ed. Christopher Pawling. New York: St. Martin's, 1984: 185–211. Burroughs's techniques and place in tradition of fantasy.

Guzlowski, John Z. "The Family in the Fiction of William Burroughs," *Midwest Quarterly* 30.1 (Autumn 1988): 11–26. Burroughs's sense of the family as a means of social control.

Hassan, Ihab. "The Literature of Silence: From Henry Miller to Beckett and Burroughs," *Encounter* 28.1 (January 1967): 74–82. Silence as deliverance/redemption for Burroughs.

Select Bibliography

———— . "The Novel of Outrage: A Minority Voice in Postwar American Fiction," *American Scholar* 34.2 (Spring 1965): 239–53. Compares Burroughs and his apocalyptic vision, his nihilism, with other writers.

———— . "The Subtracting Machine: The Work of William S. Burroughs," *Critique* 6 (Spring 1963): 4–23. Burroughs as radical utopian and nihilist, paradoxically using language to undermine its control.

Hilfer, Anthony Channell. "Mariner and Wedding Guest in William Burroughs' *Naked Lunch*," *Criticism* 22 (1980): 252–65. Burroughs's attitudes toward his reader, whom he would transform while warning the reader to be on guard.

McConnell, Frank D. "William Burroughs and the Literature of Addiction," *Massachusetts Review* 8 (1967): 665–80. Burroughs's opinions on addiction compared with opinions of De Quincey, Coleridge, Algren, etc.

Russell, Charles. "Individual Voice in the Collective Discourse: Literary Innovation in Postmodern American Fiction," *Substance: A Review of Theory and Literary Criticism* 27 (1980): 29–39. Argues that Burroughs offers "the most graphic and extreme expression of anarchic idealism and rage in contemporary literature."

Skau, Michael. "The Central Verbal System: The Prose of William Burroughs," *Style* 15.4 (1981): 401–14. Burroughs's cut-ups, theory of language.

Skerl, Jennie. "William S. Burroughs: Pop Artist," *Sphinx* 11 (1980): 1–15. Burroughs's borrowings from popular culture.

Stull, William L. "The Quest and the Question: Cosmology and Myth in the Work of William S. Burroughs, 1953–60," *Twentieth Century Literature* 24.2 (Summer 1978): 225–42. Demonstrates that Burroughs's myth is rooted in traditional quest narrative.

Weinstein, Arnold. "Freedom and Control in the Erotic Novel: The Classical *Liaisons dangereuses* versus the Surrealist *Naked*

Lunch,'' *Dada/Surrealism* 10/11 (1982): 29–38. Shows how both novels examine sexual victimization and power that erodes the self.

Works by Gregory Corso
Books

The Vestal Lady on Brattle and Other Poems. Cambridge, MA: Richard Brukenfeld, 1955.

Gasoline/The Vestal Lady on Brattle. San Francisco: City Lights, 1958.

A Pulp Magazine for the Dead Generation, with Hank Marsman. Paris: Dead Language Press, 1959.

The Happy Birthday of Death. New York: New Directions, 1960.

Minutes to Go, with William Burroughs, Brion Gysin, and Sinclair Beiles. Paris: Two Cities, 1960; San Francisco: Beach, 1964.

The American Express. Paris: Olympia, 1961.

Junge Amerikanische Lyrik, ed. with Walter Höllerer. Munich: Carl Hanser, 1961.

The Minicab War, with Anselm Hollo and Tom Raworth. London: Matrix, 1961.

Penguin Modern Poets 5, with Lawrence Ferlinghetti and Allen Ginsberg. Harmondsworth, U.K.: Penguin, 1963.

Long Live Man. New York: New Directions, 1962.

Selected Poems. London: Eyre and Spottiswoode, 1962.

The Mutation of the Spirit: A Shuffle Poem. New York: Death, 1964.

There Is Yet Time to Run Through Life and Expiate All That's Been Sadly Done. New York: New Directions, 1965.

The Geometric Poem. Milan; Fernanda Pivano, 1966.

10 Times a Poem. New York: Poets, 1967.

Elegiac Feelings American. New York: New Directions, 1970.

Egyptian Cross. New York: Phoenix Book Shop, 1971.

Select Bibliography

Ankh. New York: Phoenix Book Shop, 1971.

Poems. New York: Phoenix Book Shop, 1971.

The Night Last Was at Its Nightest. New York: Phoenix Book Shop, 1972.

Earth Egg. New York: Unmuzzled Ox, 1974.

Way Out: A Poem in Discord. Kathmandu: Bardo Matrix, 1974.

Herald of the Autochthonic Spirit. New York: New Directions, 1981.

Writings from Ox, ed. Michael Andre. New York: Unmuzzled Ox, 1981.

Mindfield: New & Selected Poems. New York: Thunder's Mouth, 1989.

Selected Uncollected Works

"In This Hung-Up Age," *Encounter* 18 (January 1962): 83–90.

"Standing on a Street-Corner," *Evergreen Review* 6 (March/April 1962): 63–78.

"Between Childhood and Manhood," *Cavalier* 15.1 (January 1965): 36–37, 39, 89–92.

"Some of My Beginning . . . and What I Feel Right Now," *Poets on Poetry*, ed. Howard Nemerov. New York: Basic, 1966: 172–81.

"That Little Black Door on the Left," *Pardon Me, Sir, but Is My Eye Hurting Your Elbow?*, ed. Bob Booker and George Foster. New York: Geis, 1967: 151–63.

Interviews

Andre, Michael. "An Interview with Gregory Corso," *Unmuzzled Ox* 22 (Winter 1981): 123–58.

(See also *Riverside Interviews 3: Gregory Corso*, below.)

Works about Corso

Bibliography

Wilson, Robert A. *A Bibliography of Works by Gregory Corso, 1954–1965*. New York: Phoenix Book Shop, 1966.

Book

Stephenson, Gregory. *Exiled Angel: A Study of the Work of Gregory Corso*. London: Hearing Eye, 1989. General analysis of the work by Corso's most perceptive critic to date.

Special Journal Issue

Riverside Interviews 3: Gregory Corso (1982). Includes Gavin Selerie, "Introduction" and "The Interview [with Gregory Corso]"; Jim Burns, "Gregory Corso: An Essay"; and Michael Horovitz, "On the Beat with Gregory Corso."

Sections of Books

Cherkovski, Neeli. "*Revolutionary of the Spirit:* Gregory Corso," *Whitman's Wild Children*. Venice and San Francisco: Lapis, 1988: 171–95. Memoir with insights into Corso's writing process.

Howard, Richard. "Gregory Corso," *Along with America: Essays on the Art of Poetry in the United States Since 1950*, enlarged ed. New York: Atheneum, 1980: 76–83. Corso as a powerful but in some ways primitive poet.

Articles

Beyle, Bill, "Gregory Corso: Introductory Shot," *Unmuzzled Ox Magazine* 22 (Winter 1981): 73–78. General commentary; Corso as a "naive" poet often speaking from a child's perspective.

Dullea, Gerard. "Ginsberg and Corso: Image and Imagination," *Thoth* 2 (Winter 1971): 17–27. Discusses Corso as a traditional, romantic poet, less innovative than Ginsberg.

Works by Allen Ginsberg

Books

Howl and Other Poems. San Francisco: City Lights, 1956.

Kaddish and Other Poems: 1958–1960. San Francisco: City Lights, 1961.

Select Bibliography

Empty Mirror: Early Poems. New York: Totem/Corinth, 1961.

Reality Sandwiches: 1953–1960. San Francisco: City Lights, 1963.

The Yage Letters, with William S. Burroughs. San Francisco: City Lights, 1963.

T. V. Baby Poems. London: Cape Goliard, 1967; New York: Grossman, 1968.

Angkor Wat. London: Fulcrum, 1968.

Planet News: 1961–1967. San Francisco: City Lights, 1968.

Airplane Dreams: Compositions from Journals. Toronto: Anansi, 1968; San Francisco: City Lights, 1969.

Indian Journals, March 1962–May 1963: Notebooks, Diary, Blank Pages, Writings. San Francisco: Dave Haselwood/City Lights, 1970.

The Fall of America: Poems of These States: 1965–1971. San Francisco: City Lights, 1972.

The Gates of Wrath: Rhymed Poems: 1948–1952. Bolinas, CA: Grey Fox, 1972.

Iron Horse. Toronto: Coach House, 1972.

Allen Verbatim: Lectures on Poetry, Politics, Consciousness, ed. Gordon Ball. New York: McGraw-Hill, 1974.

The Visions of the Great Rememberer. Amherst, MA: Mulch, 1974.

Chicago Trial Testimony. San Francisco: City Lights, 1975.

First Blues: Rags, Ballads, and Harmonium Songs: 1971–1974. New York: Full Court, 1975.

As Ever: The Collected Correspondence of Allen Ginsberg and Neal Cassady, ed. Barry Gifford. Berkeley, CA: Creative Arts, 1977.

Journals: Early Fifties, Early Sixties, ed. Gordon Ball. New York: Grove, 1977.

Mind Breaths: Poems 1972–1977. San Francisco: City Lights, 1978.

Poems All Over the Place: Mostly Seventies. Cherry Valley, NY: Cherry Valley, 1978.

Composed on the Tongue, ed. Donald Allen. Bolinas, CA: Grey Fox, 1980.

Straight Heart's Delight: Love Poems and Selected Letters: 1947–1980, with Peter Orlovsky, ed. Winston Leyland. San Francisco: Gay Sunshine, 1980.

Plutonian Ode and Other Poems: 1977–1980. San Francisco: City Lights, 1982.

Collected Poems: 1947–1980. New York: Harper and Row, 1984.

Howl: Original Draft Facsimile, ed. Barry Miles. New York: Harper and Row, 1986.

White Shroud: Poems 1980–1985. New York: Harper and Row, 1986.

Selected Uncollected Works

"An Exposition of William Carlos Williams' Poetics," *Loka 2: A Journal from the Naropa Institute.* Garden City, NY: Doubleday, 1976: 123–40.

"May Days 1988," *Broadway 2: A Poets and Painters Anthology,* ed. James Schuyler and Charles North. Brooklyn: Hanging Loose, 1989: 47–9.

"Notes for *Howl and Other Poems,*" "Introduction to *Gasoline,*" " 'When the Mode of the Music Changes the Walls of the City Shake,' " "Poetry, Violence, and the Trembling Lambs," "Prose Contribution to Cuban Revolution," "How *Kaddish* Happened," "Some Metamorphoses of Personal Poetry," and "On Improvised Poetics." *The Poetics of the New American Poetry,* ed. Donald Allen and Warren Tallman. New York: Grove, 1973: 318–50.

"Williams in a World of Objects." *William Carlos Williams: Man and Poet,* ed. Carroll F. Terrell. Orono, ME: National Poetry Foundation, 1983: 33–39.

Select Bibliography

Interviews

Cargas, Harry J. "An Interview with Allen Ginsberg," *Nimrod* 19.1 (Fall/Winter 1974): 24–29.

Carroll, Paul. "*Playboy* Interview," *Playboy* 16.4 (April 1969): 81–92, 236–44.

Clark, Thomas. "Allen Ginsberg: An Interview," *Paris Review* 37 (Spring 1966): 12–55.

Colbert, Alison, and Anita Box. "Conversations: A Talk with Allen Ginsberg," *Partisan Review* 38.3 (1971): 289–309.

Faas, Ekbert. "Allen Ginsberg," *Towards a New American Poetics.* Santa Barbara: Black Sparrow, 1979: 269–88. Preceded by an extensive essay by Faas on Ginsberg's poetry and poetics.

Freifeld, Elazar. "Conversation with Allen Ginsberg," *Tel Aviv Review* 2 (Fall/Winter 1989–90): 307–14.

Geneson, Paul. "A Conversation with Allen Ginsberg," *Chicago Review* 27.1 (Summer 1975): 27–35.

Ginsberg, Allen. "Ginsberg," *Intrepid.* 18/19 (1971): 52–61. Ginsberg interviewing himself.

Goodwin, Michael, Richard Hyatt, and Ed Ward. "Q: How Does Allen Ginsberg Write Poetry?—A: By Polishing His Mind," *City Magazine* 7.52 (13–26 November 1974): 30–34.

Koch, Kenneth. "Allen Ginsberg Talks About Poetry," *New York Times Book Review,* 23 October 1977: 9, 44–46.

Ossman, David. "Allen Ginsberg," *The Sullen Art: Interviews.* New York: Corinth, 1963: 87–95.

Rodman, Selden. "Allen Ginsberg," *Tongues of Fallen Angels.* New York: New Directions, 1974: 183–99.

Packard, William. "Allen Ginsberg," *The Poet's Craft: Interviews from "The New York Quarterly."* New York: Paragon, 1987: 30–51.

Portugés, Paul. "An Interview with Allen Ginsberg," *Boston University Journal* 25.1 (1977) : 47–59.

Portugés, Paul, and Guy Amirthanaygam. "Buddhist Meditation and Poetic Spontaneity," *Writers in East-West Encounters: New*

Cultural Bearings, ed. Guy Amirthanayagam. London: Macmillan, 1982: 10–31.

Steward, Robert, and Rebekah Presson. "Sacred Speech: A Conversation with Allen Ginsberg," *New Letters* 54.1 (Fall 1987): 72–86.

Tytell, John. "Conversation with Allen Ginsberg," *Partisan Review* 41.3 (Summer 1974): 253–62.

Young, Allen. "Allen Ginsberg," *Gay Sunshine Interviews*, ed. Winston Leyland. San Francisco: Gay Sunshine, 1978: 95–128.

Works about Ginsberg
Bibliographies

Dowden, George. *A Bibliography of Works by Allen Ginsberg: October, 1943 to July 1, 1967*. San Francisco: City Lights, 1971.

Kraus, Michelle P. *Allen Ginsberg: An Annotated Bibliography, 1969–1977*. Metuchen, NJ, and London: Scarecrow, 1980.

Biographies

Kramer, Jane. *Allen Ginsberg in America*. New York: Random House, 1969. Admiring portrait; originally *New Yorker* profile.

Miles, Barry. *Ginsberg: A Biography*. New York and London: Simon and Schuster, 1989. The principal source for information on Ginsberg's life.

Books

Burns, Glen. *Great Poets Howl: A Study of Allen Ginsberg's Poetry, 1943–1955*. Frankfurt am Main: Peter Lang, 1983. Major study of the early development of Ginsberg's poetry and poetics.

Hyde, Lewis, ed. *On the Poetry of Allen Ginsberg*. Ann Arbor: University of Michigan Press, 1984. An excellent cross section of commentary on Ginsberg's work and interviews with the poet.

Select Bibliography

Merrill, Thomas F. *Allen Ginsberg*, rev. ed. Boston: Twayne, 1988.

Mottram, Eric. *Allen Ginsberg in the Sixties.* Brighton, U. K.: Unicorn Bookshop, 1972. Close reading of "Wichita Vortex Sutra," "Angkor Wat," and other poems from the decade.

Portugés, Paul. *The Visionary Poetics of Allen Ginsberg.* Santa Barbara: Ross-Erikson, 1978. The Blake visions, drugs, and Ginsberg's work; an important study.

Sections of Books

Breslin, James E. "Allen Ginsberg's 'Howl,' " *From Modern to Contemporary.* Chicago: University of Chicago Press, 1984: 77–109. The poem and its genesis interpreted in a largely biographical context.

Breslin, Paul. "Allen Ginsberg as Representative Man: The Road to Naropa," *The Psycho-Political Muse: American Poetry Since the Fifties.* Chicago: University of Chicago Press, 1987: 22–41. Sees Ginsberg working at intersection of public and private experience; his understanding of madness and poetry as prophecy.

Géfin, Laszlo. "Ellipsis and Riprap: The Ideograms of Ginsberg and Snyder," *Ideogram: History of a Poetic Method.* Austin: University of Texas Press, 1982: 117–34. Ellipses in Ginsberg's poetry as part of a twentieth-century tradition.

Howard, Richard. "Allen Ginsberg," *Alone with America: Essays on the Art of Poetry in the United States Since 1950*, enlarged ed. New York: Atheneum, 1980: 176–83. Ginsberg as prophetic poet.

Mersmann, James F. *Out of the Vietnam Vortex: A Study of Poets and Poetry Against the War.* Lawrence: University of Kansas Press, 1974: 31–75. Ginsberg's antiwar poetry.

Molesworth, Charles. "Republican Objects and Utopian Moments: The Poetry of Robert Lowell and Allen Ginsberg." *The Fierce Embrace.* Columbia: University of Missouri Press, 1979: 37–60. Explores Ginsberg's attempt to create an intense poetry of sensation.

Perloff, Marjorie. "A Lion in Our Living Room: Reading Allen Ginsberg in the Eighties," *Poetic License: Essays on Modernist and Postmodernist Lyric*. (Evanston, IL: Northwestern University Press, 1990): 199–230. Reaffirmation of Ginsberg's stature at a time when politics and poetics seem to be moving in a conservative direction opposite to his own.

Rosenthal, M. L. "Allen Ginsberg," *The New Poets: American and British Poetry Since World War II*. New York: Oxford University Press, 1967: 89–112. Ginsberg as a confessional poet.

Rosenthal, M. L., and Sally M. Gall. *The Modern Poetic Sequence: The Genius of Modern Poetry*. New York: Oxford University Press, 1983: 422–28. The authors claim that "Kaddish" not sufficiently developed but an important example of the "poetic sequence."

Simpson, Louis. "The Eye Altering Alters All," *A Revolution in Taste: Studies of Dylan Thomas, Allen Ginsberg, Sylvia Plath, and Robert Lowell*. New York: Macmillan, 1978: 45–82. A general study of Ginsberg's work by a poet working in a very different tradition.

Articles

Aiken, William. "Denise Levertov, Robert Duncan, and Allen Ginsberg: Modes of the Self in Projective Poetry." *Modern Poetry Studies* 10.2/3 (1981): 200–45. Ginsberg's Vietnam poetry compared with Levertov's and Duncan's.

Breslin, James. "Allen Ginsberg: The Origins of 'Howl' and 'Kaddish'" *Iowa Review* 8.2 (Spring 1977): 82–108. Psychological examination of Ginsberg in context of older authority figures.

Dougherty, Jay. "From Society to Self: Ginsberg's Inward Turn in *Mind Breaths*," *Sagetrieb* 6.1 (Spring 1987): 81–92. Traces development of contemplative mode in Ginsberg's work.

Heffernan, James. "Politics and Freedom: Refractions of Blake in Joyce Cary and Allen Ginsberg," *Romantic and Modern*, ed.

Select Bibliography

George Bornstein. Pittsburgh: University of Pittsburgh Press, 1977. Influence of Blake as prophet on Ginsberg.

Hunsberger, Bruce. "Kit Smart's Howl," *Wisconsin Studies in Contemporary Literature* 6 (Winter/Spring 1965): 34–44. Influence of Smart as a religious visionary on Ginsberg.

Johnson, Mark. "Discovery as Technique: Allen Ginsberg's 'These States'," *Contemporary Poetry* 4.2 (1981): 23–46. Form in Ginsberg's poetics emerges in the process of writing.

Lyon, George W., Jr. "Allen Ginsberg: Angel Headed Hipster," *Journal of Popular Culture* 3.3 (Winter 1969): 391–403. Ginsberg as mystic with a vision centered in the self; importance of Jewish mysticism to his work.

Peck, John. "Pollution, Purification and Song," *Tri-Quarterly* 75 (Spring/Summer 1989): 121–48. Ginsberg's Vietnam-era poetry.

Pinckney, Darryl. "The May King," *Parnassus: Poetry in Review* 10.1 (Spring/Summer 1982): 99–116. Ginsberg as visionary and love poet.

Portugés, Paul. "Allen Ginsberg's Paul Cézanne and the *Pater Omnipotens Aeterna Deus*," *Contemporary Literature* 21 (Summer 1980): 435–49. Cézanne's influence on Ginsberg's poetics.

Works by Jack Kerouac

Books

The Town and the City. New York: Harcourt, Brace, 1950; London: Eyre and Spottiswoode, 1951.

On the Road. New York: Viking 1957; London: Deutsch, 1958.

The Subterraneans. New York: Grove, 1958; London: Deutsch, 1960.

The Dharma Bums. New York: Viking, 1958; London: Deutsch, 1959.

Doctor Sax: Faust Part Three. New York: Grove, 1959; London: Deutsch, 1977.

Maggie Cassidy. New York: Avon, 1959; London: Panther, 1960.

Mexico City Blues. New York: Grove, 1959.

The Scripture of the Golden Eternity. New York: Totem/Corinth, 1960; London: Centaur, 1960.

Tristessa. New York: Avon, 1960; London: World, 1963.

Lonesome Traveler. New York: McGraw-Hill, 1960; London: Deutsch, 1963.

Book of Dreams. San Francisco: City Lights, 1961.

Pull My Daisy. New York: Grove, 1961; London: Evergreen, 1961.

Big Sur. New York: Farrar, Straus and Cudahy, 1962; London: Deutsch, 1963.

Visions of Gerard. New York: Farrar, Straus, 1963; London: Deutsch, 1964.

Desolation Angels. New York: Coward-McCann, 1965; London: Deutsch, 1966.

Satori in Paris. New York: Grove, 1966; London: Deutsch, 1967.

Vanity of Duluoz: An Adventurous Education, 1935–1946. New York: Coward-McCann, 1968; London: Deutsch, 1969.

Scattered Poems, ed. Ann Charters. San Francisco: City Lights, 1971.

Pic. New York: Grove, 1971; London: Deutsch, 1973.

Visions of Cody. New York: McGraw-Hill, 1972; London: Deutsch, 1973.

Trip Trap: Haiku Along the Road from San Francisco to New York. Bolinas, CA: Grey Fox, 1973.

Heaven & Other Poems, ed. Donald Allen. San Francisco: Grey Fox, 1977.

Kerouac's Last Word: Jack Kerouac in Escapade, ed. Tom Clark. Sudbury, MA: Water Row, 1986.

Interviews

Berrigan, Ted. "Jack Kerouac," *On the Road: Text and Criticism,* ed. Scott Donaldson. New York: Viking, 1979: 538–72.

Select Bibliography

Scesny, Diana. "Jack Kerouac at Northport," *Athanor* 1.1 (1971): 1–17; 1.2 (1971): 1–15; 1.3 (1972), 1–24.

Tallmer, Jerry. "Jack Kerouac: Back to the Village—But Still on the Road," *The Village Voice Reader,* ed. Daniel Wolf and Edwin Fancher. New York: Grove, 1963: 32–34.

Works about Kerouac

Bibliographies

Carters, Ann. *A Bibliography of Works by Jack Kerouac, 1939–1975,* rev. ed. New York: Phoenix Bookshop, 1975.

Milewski, Robert J. *Jack Kerouac: An Annotated Bibliography of Secondary Sources, 1944–1979.* Metuchen, NJ, and London: Scarecrow, 1981.

Biographies

Cassady, Carolyn. *Heat Beat: My Life with Jack and Neal.* Berkeley, CA: Creative Arts, 1976; *Off the Road: My Years with Cassady, Kerouac, and Ginsberg.* New York: Morrow, 1990. Memoirs; important biographical sources.

Charters, Ann. *Kerouac.* San Francisco: Straight Arrow, 1972. The first Kerouac biography and still a major source.

Clark, Tom. *Jack Kerouac.* San Diego: Harcourt Brace Jovanovich, 1984. Concise, well-written biography. The best introduction to Kerouac.

Gifford, Barry, and Lawrence Lee. *Jack's Book: An Oral Biography of Jack Kerouac.* New York: St. Martin's, 1978. Liberally quotes from interviews with Kerouac's associates and friends.

Johnson, Joyce. *Minor Characters.* New York: Houghton Mifflin, 1983. Memoir by a woman who lived with Kerouac.

McNally, Dennis. *Desolate Angel: Jack Kerouac, the Beats, and America.* New York: Random House, 1979. Sees Kerouac in terms of political and social developments of the era.

Montgomery, John. *Kerouac West Coast*. Palo Alto: Fels and Firn, 1976. Memoir of Kerouac by the writer on whom he modeled Henry Morley in *The Dharma Bums*.

Nicosia, Gerald. *Memory Babe: A Critical Biography of Jack Kerouac*. New York: Grove, 1983. The most detailed and authoritative biography but critical commentary is at times disappointing.

Books

Beaulieu, Victor-Lévy. *Jack Kerouac: A Chicken Essay*, trans. Sheila Fischman. Toronto: Coach House, 1975. Impressionistic essay on Kerouac as a French-Canadian.

Challis, Chris. *Quest for Kerouac*. London: Faber and Faber, 1984. Autobiography; an Englishman's attempt to come to terms with Kerouac's works and legend; accounts of visits to places and people associated with Kerouac.

Donaldson, Scott, ed. *On the Road: Text and Criticism*. New York: Viking, 1979. Provides a selection of the critical work on Kerouac and reprints Kerouac's "The Origins of the Beat Generation" and "Essentials of Spontaneous Prose."

French, Warren G. *Jack Kerouac*. Boston: Twayne, 1986. Kerouac as a divided writer suggested by the differences between Peter and Francis in *The Town and the City*. French prefers Francis.

Gaffié, Luc. *Jack Kerouac: The New Picaroon*. New York: Postillion, 1977. Kerouac as picaresque novelist.

Ginsberg, Allen. *The Visions of the Great Rememberer*. Amherst, MA: Mulch, 1974. Memoir and commentary expanded from introduction to *Visions of Cody*.

Hipkiss, Robert A. *Jack Kerouac: Prophet of a New Romanticism*. Lawrence: Regents Press of Kansas, 1976. A study of the Duluoz saga with negative criticism of *Visions of Gerard, Visions of Cody, Tristessa,* and the poetry.

Select Bibliography

Huebel, Harry R. *Jack Kerouac.* Boise: Western Writers Series, 1979. Good general survey with emphasis on Kerouac's sense of the West.

Hunt, Timothy A. *Kerouac's Crooked Road: Development of a Fiction.* Hamden, CT: Archon, 1981. *On the Road* was (with *Visions of Cody, Pic,* and so forth) only one of Kerouac's several attempts to deal with Neal Cassady in fiction.

Montgomery, John, comp. *The Kerouac We Knew: Unposed Portraits, Action Shots.* Kentfield, CA: Fels and Firn, 1982; *Kerouac at the "Wild Boar" & Other Skirmishes.* San Anselmo, CA: Fels and Firn, 1986. Memoirs and commentary by sympathetic critics and friends.

Walsh, Joy. *Jack Kerouac: Statement in Brown.* Clarence Center, NY: Textile Bridge, 1984. Miscellaneous critical commentary and observations by respected Kerouac scholar and editor of *Moody Street Irregulars.*

Weinreich, Regina. *The Aesthetics of Spontaneity: A Study of the Fiction of Jack Kerouac.* Carbondale: Southern Illinois University Press, 1987. Major study of the development of Kerouac's writing theories and practice.

Journals Devoted to Kerouac and the Beats

Kerouac Connection. (1984–)
Moody Street Irregulars: A Jack Kerouac Newsletter. (1978–)
(Both journals publish serious commentary on Kerouac and the Beats. The first is British, the second American.)

Special Journal Issue

Review of Contemporary Fiction 3.2 (Summer 1983). Includes, among other pieces, William Crawford Woods, "'A New Field': A Note on *The Dharma Bums*" (positive reevaluation of *The Dharma Bums*); Larry Kart, "Jack Kerouac's 'Jazz America' or Who Was Roger Beloit?" (influence of jazz on Kerouac's prose); Joy Walsh, "Kerouac's Harmonious

Combination of Elements: The Long Symphonic Sentence"
(musical qualities of Kerouac's prose); Jim Burns, "Kerouac
and Jazz" (Kerouac's taste in, and knowledge of, jazz); Eric
Mottram, "A Preface to *Visions of Cody*" (important analysis
of myths, backgrounds, etc., contributing to the book); Regina
Weinreich, "The Brothers Martin or the Decline of America"
(*The Town and the City* and Kerouac's disillusionment with the
American dream); George Dardess, "The 'Marvels' of Gerard" (transformation of memory to fiction).

Articles

Allen, Eliot D. "That Was No Lady—That Was Jack Kerouac's
Girl," *Essays in Modern American Literature,* ed. Richard E.
Langford. Deland, FL: Steton University Press, 1963: 97–102.
Argues that Kerouac represents women as oversexed and
inarticulate.

Blackburn, William. "Han Shan Gets Drunk with the Butchers:
Kerouac's Buddhism in *On the Road, The Dharma Bums,* and
Desolation Angels," *Literature East and West* 21.1–4 (January–December 1977); 9–22. Considers Sal Paradise's quest as
an exemplification of the Buddhist search for enlightenment.

Charters, Ann. "Kerouac's Literary Method and Experiments:
The Evidence of the Manuscript Notebooks in the Berg Collection," *Bulletin of Research in the Humanities* 84.4 (Winter
1981): 431–50. Reviews Kerouac's notebooks to show that he
did revise sometimes.

Dardess, George. "The Delicate Dynamics of Friendship: A Reconsideration of Jack Kerouac's *On the Road,*" *American Literature* 46 (May 1974): 200–6. Changes in Sal's friendship
with Dean are seen as structuring the novel.

——— . "The Logic of Spontaneity: A Reconsideration of Kerouac's 'Spontaneous Prose Method,'" *Boundary 2* 3.3 (1975):
729–43. Defends Kerouac's aesthetics of spontaneity as within
American tradition.

Select Bibliography

D'Orso, Michael. "Man Out of Time: Kerouac, Spengler, and the 'Faustian Soul,' " *Studies in American Fiction* 11.1 (Spring 1983): 19–30. Traces the influence of Spengler's *The Decline of the West* on Kerouac.

Gussow, Adam. "Bohemia Revisited: Malcolm Cowley, Jack Kerouac, and *On the Road*," *Georgia Review* 38.2 (Summer 1984): 291–311. Discusses the editing of *On the Road;* sympathetic to Cowley's role.

McNally, Dennis. "Prophets on the Burning Shore: Jack Kerouac, Gary Snyder, and San Francisco." *A Literary History of the American West* [no editor listed]. Fort Worth: Texas Christian University Press, 1987): 482–95. Depicts Kerouac and Snyder's shared disaffection with western civilization.

Sorrell, Richard S. "Novelists and Ethnicity: Jack Kerouac and Grace Metalious as Franco-Americans," *MELUS* 9.1 (Spring 1982): 37–52. Examines the influence of Kerouac's French-Canadian heritage on his work.

Tallman, Warren. "Kerouac's Sound," *Tamarack Review* 11 (Spring 1959): 58–74. Exceptionally important essay dealing with the influence of hipster culture and bop on Kerouac's prose.

INDEX

Abbott, Keith: "Ballad of Jack Kerouac's 1957," xi
Allen, Donald: *The New American Poetry,* 193
All the Fine Young Cannibals, 13
Anderson, Laurie, 24, 198 n. 5
Anderson, Sherwood, 16, 17, 18, 45; *Winesburg, Ohio,* 35
Ansen, Alan, 1, 19, 166
Apollinaire, Guillaume, 101
Artaud, Antonin, 101, 103, 134
Ashbery, John, 114
Auden, W. H.: *The Age of Anxiety,* 13

Baraka, Amiri, 3, 190
Barth, John, 4
Barthes, Roland, 195
Baudelaire, Charles, 95, 134
Beat Generation, 3, 7–8, 11
The Beats: and Beat Generation, 3; as celebrities, xi, xii; and expres-
    sionism, 14–19; and hipsters, xiii, 5–6, 8–9, 12–14; influence
    on other writers, 190–93; as New Yorkers, 4, 6–7; as opponents
    of materialistic, conformist American culture, xii, 8–9, 10, 12–
    13, 40; and poetics of voice, 193–95; and San Francisco Renais-
    sance, 2–3; and spiritual quest, 11, 196–97; and women, 22–24;
    as writers, xii–xiii, 1, 12, 14–19, 193–97. *See also* Burroughs,
    William S.; Corso, Gregory; Ginsberg, Allen; Kerouac, Jack
Beckett, Samuel: *Waiting for Godot,* 158
Beiles, Sinclair, 139, 166
Bellow, Saul, 4
Berrigan, Ted, 39, 60, 61
Berryman, John, 131

Index

Index

Index

Index

Index

Index

Index

Index

Printed in the United States
126429LV00001BA/21/A